LEARNING FROM

Isaiah

AMANDA NORTHROP

WESTBOW
PRESS®
A DIVISION OF THOMAS NELSON
& ZONDERVAN

WestBow Press books may be ordered through booksellers or by contacting:

WestBow Press
A Division of Thomas Nelson & Zondervan
1663 Liberty Drive
Bloomington, IN 47403
www.westbowpress.com
844-714-3454

ISBN: 978-1-6642-9382-3 (sc)
ISBN: 978-1-6642-9381-6 (e)

Library of Congress Control Number: 2023903756

Print information available on the last page.

WestBow Press rev. date: 03/14/2023

Some of the material in this book is excerpted from Chronological Life Application Study Bible, New Living Translation (NLT).

Contents

Chapter 1

INTRODUCTION

An interesting book in the Old Testament is the book of Isaiah. It is easy to overlook due to its location in the bible and is not easy to read. Isaiah is the first book of the Old Testament that is often called the prophets but it is not the first one written. It is located after some of the easiest and most enjoyable books to read: Psalms, Proverbs, Ecclesiastes, and The Song of Solomon. While Isaiah continues a message of hope, it is mixed with visions of misery which are harder to read. You can see its importance in how much it is used in the New Testament. New Testament writers use Isaiah's works throughout the New Testament to show that God keeps his promises and has provided salvation for us.

Isaiah has a multitude of verses that are wide known, easily-quoted, and commonly used . They are wonderful verses concerning Immanuel and the coming of Jesus. Isaiah contains more than just those verses. It is a wonderful book of God's plan for Jerusalem between Isaiah's time and the coming of Jesus. If you ignore the cultural references, it provides the message of salvation and promise of a messiah. It was written with the intention that God is for all people and not just the Jewish community. The book prophesied of God's salvation being a universal blessing which is just one of the reasons that it is a great book to revisit and take a deeper look at.

A second reason to do a good read of Isaiah is that it contains lessons from history that are applicable to our current culture. The first thirty-nine chapters are poems about God's judgment upon immoral and idolatrous men. While thousands of years have passed, our society continues to do these immoral acts and worship idols that prevent us from having a fulfilling relationship with God. These first chapters show that everyone needs God's salvation. They were waiting for the Messiah and we are waiting for his return. We are both doing acts and worship that create a need for the Messiah to die on a cross so that we do not have to die for our sins.

The last reason to read Isaiah is to get a better grasp of some of the prophecies of the Messiah. Chapters forty through sixty-six contain these Messianic prophecies. Understanding when and how these prophecies were given provides a deeper appreciation for God's planning. Isaiah wrote his prophecies during his ministry from about 740 B.C. to 680 B.C. You can find so many details about the future that it is easy to forget that Isaiah spoke these details hundreds of years before Jesus's birth. God ensured that every detail and promise was fulfilled. The way that the New Testament and Isaiah connect with each other despite the vast difference in the time that they were wrote shows that God has a plan for everything. I encourage everyone to read all of Isaiah, even the difficult parts that are dark and gloomy.

Isaiah's original purpose was to call Judah back to God and inform everyone of God's plan to provide salvation through the Messiah. The northern kingdom had already been captured but Judah, the southern kingdom, was in political turmoil that was leading the kingdom away from God. The kingdom was not relying on God but was looking to other nations for security. We, individually and collectively, are on the same path. Even chrisitans tend to rely on outside forces to provide security instead of relying on God. Our society is like Judah and needs to return to God for guidance and protection.

THEMES

There are multiple themes for the book: holiness, punishment, salvation, Messiah, and hope. Isaiah's name in Hebrew is Yesha'yahu which appropriately means Yahweh is Salvation and aptly gives the main theme of his writing.

Holiness

The Greek word *hagios* is the origin of the word holy. Its meaning is "set apart" or "separated" which is where we get the concept of holiness is being set apart from sin. God is absolutely holy and is completely separated from all that is evil and morally imperfect. We are able to be holy through our relationship with him and can take the likeness of holiness when we accept the Messiah that was prophesied in Isaiah.

Punishment

Isaiah has some darker portions. Isaiah includes a list of judgments on nations of the time. These judgments were given due to the sins of the people. This included a judgment for Judah which was sinning against God. Suffering can come from sinning as punishment in an attempt to change your mind, heart, and ways.

Salvation

Isaiah proclaims that the salvation that God offers is for all people and is free, joyful, and eternal. We often see these descriptions of salvation in the New Testament, but the Old Testament was usually more traditional in its sense of God's grace.

Messiah

The Hebrew word *masiah* means "the anointed one" and parallels the Greek term *christos* or more commonly known as Christ. The book of Isaiah contains several of the messianic prophecies that are in the Old Testament. These prophecies are throughout the book of Isaiah and include a prophecy of the suffering and death on the cross that Jesus would endure hundreds of years later.

Hope

One of the largest themes of Isaiah is the offer of hope and a way to be completely forgiven. Isaiah gives multiple prophecies of the Messiah. In the end, there will be a perfect peace with no conflict. While there is no estimate of when this time of perfect peace will come, Isaiah was correct about the Messiah's coming and his suffering for us. Now we just have to wait for the perfect peace that is coming with the new heaven and new earth. When you live with hope, you have the expectation of getting the peace that Isaiah describes.

LESSONS

Our society is in a great upheaval that mimics Isaiah's society. There are many lessons from Isaiah that you can apply to your lives and learn from their mistakes. The big picture messages of Isaiah are:

- Judgment is inevitable, but people can have a special relationship with God.
- Sometimes you must suffer judgment and discipline before you are restored to God.

These messages are just as important today as they were when Isaiah first spoke them to the people of Judah. It is of note that one of the biggest questions from believers is "why do good people suffer?" Judgment and discipline are things that we tend to see as punishment and not as tools for growth. You need to change your mindset. Instead of focusing on the reason for the judgment, focus on the relationship with God and how you can grow closer to God.

ORGANIZATION

Isaiah starts with what is often called "The book of Judgment" and includes the first thirty-nine chapters. The book starts with messages of rebuke and promise for Judah. This includes charges from God against Judah, His discipline, and His promise of restoration . The majority of this portion is judgment against multiple nations including Assyria, Moab, Egypt, Babylon, and Arabia. There are chapters concerning universal judgment that is followed with deliverance and blessing. The book of judgment continues with the six woes and ends with a final judgment and promise.

The second part of Isaiah is often called "The Book of Comfort" and includes most of the Messianic prophecies. Isaiah prophesied on Israel's deliverance and restoration after exile, a Servant and his ministry, and everlasting deliverance and everlasting judgment.

Book of Judgment (1-39)

- Messages of Rebuke and Promise (1-6)
  - Intro: Charges against Judah
  - Future discipline (2-4)
  - Judgment and Exile (5)
  - Isaiah's Commission (6)

- Prophecies concerning Aramean (7-12)
- Judgment against Nations (13-23)
- Judgment and Promise (24-27)
- Six Woes
  - Woe to Ephraim
  - Woe to Jerusalem
  - Woe to those who rely on foreign alliance
  - Woe to obstinate nation
  - Woe to those who rely on Egypt
  - Woe to Assyria
- More prophecies of judgment and promise
- Historical Transition to exile

Book of Comfort (40-66)

- Deliverance and restoration of Israel (40-48)
- The Servant's Ministry and Israel's restoration (49-57)
- Everlasting Deliverance and Everlasting Judgment (58-66)

The organization of the Isaiah can be a hindrance for some people because it does start with some of the harder aspects such as judgment and punishment. Do not focus on the cultural pieces that you can use to defend why the lesson does not apply to you and instead focus on how to apply the lessons.

Chapter 2

MESSAGES OF REBUKES
AND PROMISES

ISAIAH 1-6

I saiah prophesied about divine judgment for both Israel and Judah during his time as a prophet for God. He was part of a society that was in great upheaval and uncertainty just like ours. He saw visions from God while Judah was under four different kings: Uzziah, Jotham, Ahaz, and Hezekiah. Both the northern and southern kingdoms were sinning against God by perverting justice, oppressing the poor, turning from God to idols, and looking for aid from pagan nations. Isaiah's message is an encouragement to turn to God and away from sin. It is easy to engage in the same sins and need this reminder to turn from sin to God.

The first heading for Isaiah says a lot: A Message for Rebellious Judah. But you should make it personal and call it a message for a rebellious follower. God gave a message to Isaiah that applied to Judah but also to us individually. God's message is:

> The children I raised and cared for have rebelled against me. Even an ox knows its owner, and a donkey recognizes its master's care--but Israel doesn't know its

master. My people don't recognize my care for them.
(Verses 2-3, NLT).

The people of Judah were a sinful nation. They were rejecting God, despising God, and turning their back on God. Isaiah asks, "Why do you continue to invite punishment?" and "Must you rebel forever?" God gave warnings to Judah trying to change people's minds and hearts. God's children are described as injured and sick, specifically battered from head to foot and covered with bruises, welts, and infected wounds. While Isaiah is describing the people of his time, this description applies to us too.

Isaiah describes the destruction that Judah would endure due to their sins. The warnings include the country lying in ruins, burning of town, foreigners plundering the fields before destroying everything. The people of Judah believed that being plundered by foreigners was the worst kind of judgment. God was going to punish his children with their worst judgment due to their sins. Despite the severity of God's judgment, He promised mercy and would leave a remnant and deliver His people from exile in the future.

We are told to listen to the Lord and listen to the law of our God in verse 10. God then asks for sincere faith and devotion instead of empty outward gestures. God wants His people to have their outward expressions be genuine demonstrations of inner devotion. Your actions should be for God and not society. He wants your love and trust more than empty rituals.

In verse sixteen, we are instructed to wash ourselves, be clean, and give up our evil ways. We are told to learn to do good, seek justice, help the oppressed, defend the cause of orphans, and fight for the rights of widows. These instructions are as relevant now as they were to the generations before us. You need to turn away from your sinful ways and live to do God's will.

Isaiah ends with a promise from God that he will forgive us for our sins and make us as white as wool. He will provide for us if we obey Him, but we will be devoured by our enemies if we refuse to listen. The people of Isaiah's time did not listen to this warning and endured years of exile and slavery.

Unfaithful Jerusalem

The last eleven verses of chapter one compares God's people to a prostitute due to their actions. The people of Judah were worshiping idols which is a sin that we often commit too. Their faith is described as worthless, impure, and diluted with different analogies. Leaders of the society are called rebels who love bribes and demand payoffs instead of defending the weak.

Even though the people sin against God, He promises that He will remove our sins. You can be revived by righteousness if you repent. Sinners will be completely destroyed but the Lord will save those who repent their lives to Him.

We should be ashamed of our idol worship instead of excusing or defending it. God should have your first loyalty instead of work, fame, money, or other modern day idols. If you do not turn away from your idols, you are leaving tinder that can create a fire that can destroy your life.

Chapter two starts with a vision of what is going to occur at the Temple in the last days. The temple will be the most important place on Earth. This is a similar prophecy to the one that John describes in Revelation 21. The vision describes people from all over the world streaming to the temple to worship. People will go to the temple to be taught God's will so that they can walk in his path. Isaiah 2:4 shows that in the end of days, God will mediate between nations and will settle international disputes. There will be no more war and peace will be between the nations.

Yet we do not have to wait until the end of day to hold God as a priority for our lives. You should seek his teachings and walk in his path today. While the current society lives in conflict, you can obey God and keep your eyes on his promise of an eternal reward.

A Warning of Judgment

The descendants of Jacob were called to walk in the light of the Lord in verse six of chapter two. We are called to do the same. The people of Judah were following the practices of neighboring people which included worshiping idols and practicing sorcery. They were making alliances with pagans instead of relying on God. God promises to humble the people of Judah for their actions concerning idol worship. It is best said in verse eleven:

> Human pride will be brought down, and human arrogance will be humbled. Only the Lord will be exalted on that day of judgment. (NLT)

While our idols have changed to more modern things, our human pride and arrogance still lead us to rely on our own efforts instead of on God. On the day of reckoning, God will punish the proud and mighty and the Lord will be exalted. We often put our hope and confidence in physical protection, economic prosperity, and pleasure and enjoyment instead of in God alone. On the day of reckoning, idols will be completely destroyed and the universal sovereignty of the Lord will be fully recognized.

We tend to trust other people more than we trust in God. Isaiah recognizes this and warns us of our mortality by describing humans as frail as breath. It is clearly advised to not put our trust in mere humans when we should be putting our trust in God.

Judgment against Judah

Isaiah prophesied that the Lord would take away everything that Jerusalem and Judah depend on in chapter three. This would include food, water, heroes, soldiers, judges, prophets, elders, high officials, and advisors. The Lord promised to make leaders into boys and rulers into toddlers. Verse five says that people will oppress each other--man against man, neighbor against neighbor. Young people will insult their elders, and vulgar people will sneer at the honorable. This does not only describe the society of Judah hundreds of years ago but is an accurate description of our own society. Our leaders act like children, people are quick to oppress others for their own desires, and youth do not respect their elders. A society is held together with invisible bonds of common concerns with a moral base. Internal atrophy that follows corruption and breaks the bonds of society has been used and continues to be used as a judgment from God for those who forget to rely on God. The internal atrophy is fixed when repentance is sought.

Isaiah prophesied that Jerusalem and Judah would fall because of their decision to speak against the Lord and not obey his word. Individuals were proudly provoking God with their sin and displaying their pride instead of trying to hide it. This continues to occur; people live sinful lives that appear glamorous and exciting but will lead to doom and destruction with their choices. Remember that sin will be punished by God. Instead of inviting destruction with a life of sin, you need to obey God and live for him. Isaiah prophesied the reward for the godly in verse 3:10 when he promises that all will be well for the godly and they will enjoy the rich reward they have earned. You might not see your reward until you reach heaven, but God will reward the faithful.

In Judah, the elders and rulers were supposed to help the poor as instructed by their laws. The Lord pronounced judgment on the elders and rulers. They were ruining Israel by stealing from the poor instead of helping the poor. The Lord condemns leaders for how they lead. They seek their own advantage instead of putting the needs of the poor and the masses before their own needs. You should keep this in mind in your own life when you lead others. Lets be good examples of leaders and not do as the elders and rulers.

Jerusalem's Warning

The Lord describes Jerusalem as haughty in 3:16 due to its people's love of the refined way of life. The society in Jerusalem during Isaiah's time openly displayed their proud self-reliance, power, and prestige. The people were self-serving and self-centered instead of trying to stop the oppression of the poor. We are meant to use what God provides us to help others instead of flaunting it. Our own society is having this issue currently. People with resources are more focused on flaunting their "success" or "status" instead of helping others.

The Lord prophesied that he would strip away everything that makes Jerusalem beautiful. In the end, the men will die in battle and the city would be thrown into mourning. Our own society is going in a similar path.

A Promise of Restoration

The Lord promises to restore Jerusalem with the branch of the Lord which is most likely a reference to the Messiah. This branch will be beautiful and glorious. The Lord will cleanse Zion of its filth and bloodstains with the hot breath of fiery judgment. Lord promises to protect Zion and the remaining followers after Zion is purified and restored.

A Song about the Lord's Vineyard

The vineyard in chapter five is Israel and God's chosen people. While God's intention for Israel was to be his chosen nation and carry out God's plan to uphold justice, it had instead bore bad fruit. God did all the work to start a good fruit by plowing the land, clearing the stones, and planting the best vines. The Lord built a watchtower to protect the vineyard and a winepress to be used to create wine. But instead of sweet grapes, Israel grew bitter grapes. The Lord did everything necessary to grow sweet grapes, but the actions of the people were evil.

While the Lord expected a crop of justice and righteousness, the people of Judah were oppressing others and being violent. In response to a bad fruit, God would tear down the hedges and break down the walls so that the vineyard could become a wild place with no rain and produce no more fruit.

Judah's Guilt and Judgment

The Lord condemns six specific sins of Israel and Judah. The six sins are exploiting others, drunkenness, taking pride in sin, confusing moral standards, being conceited, and perverting justice. God had punished the northern kingdom of Israel with destruction by Assyria due to these sins. The southern kingdom of Judah was going down a similar path with their sins during Isaiah's time.

The word exploit as a verb is defined as to use someone or something, usually selfishly or for profit. When people exploit others, they use either an individual or an item to gain a personal advantage. In Isaiah's time, this was done by evicting others from homes and fields so that an individual could own an unfair amount of land in an attempt to produce more wine for more profit. God promised that when many homes stood deserted due to exploitation, the vineyards gained by exploitation will produce little profit. Today's exploitations can be a wide variety of actions where an individual selfishly uses others for their own gain. While we do not see God's punishment of individuals most of the time, God does promise to ensure that they are punished.

The next sin that God condemned was drunkenness. People would spend most of the day drinking and partying instead of working. Sadly, this sin is still widely practiced. Instead of focusing on the Lord and his work, people pursue their own pleasure with alcohol and other pleasurable activities that God provided us. Drunkenness is a sin that demonstrates how we stray from the Lord when we pursue pleasures and enjoyment that are appropriate in moderation but are an issue in excess. Drinking in excess leads to ignoring or exploiting the needs of others. While God wants you to enjoy life, he does not want you to engage in activities that lead you away from him. When you stray from God, the pleasures that you indulge in can lead to the cause of our destruction. We can see this today when an individual who drank for years dies of liver cancer or similar disease.

The sin of taking pride in sin is seen when an individual is arrogant in their sin and proudly displays it. In the verse Isaiah 5:19 it says "They even mock God and say, "Hurry up and do something! We want to see what you can do. Let the Holy One of Israel carry out his plan, for we want to know what it is."" We should not see our sin as a badge of honor, nor should we proclaim our sin with arrogance. The next sin of confusing moral standards is seen as saying "that evil is good and good is evil, that dark is light and light is dark, that bitter is sweet and sweet is bitter" in verse twenty. Our own society is having an issue with this sin due to a reluctance to respect firm definitions of moral issues. Instead of having clear distinctions on moral values, society is promoting a fluid view of morality that is causing moral confusion. We need to go back to the moral values established in the bible instead of following society's example.

The last two sins mentioned are conceit and perverting justice. Verse 21 defines conceit as being wise in their own eyes and thinking themselves so clever. We often think of conceit as excessive pride. You can see conceit in our current society. Individuals who pervert justice are those who take bribes and then do not let justice prevail or those who punish the innocent instead of the wicked. These individuals will suffer due to their rejection of God's law. Make it your priority to understand and obey God's word to ensure that you do not commit these sins.

Isaiah informed Judah that God would punish them if they did not repent from their sins. Every sin has consequences. Judah's consequence for their sin was invasion by another nation instead of continued protection from the Lord. The judgment for sin is often not immediate and takes time, often years, before God will act against his children. You should not test God's patience but should be obedient in your lives.

Isaiah's Cleansing and Call

According to Chapter 6, Isaiah received his vision and was called to ministry about 740 B.C. This vision came in the year that King Uzziah died. While King Uzziah was a good king except for a few small issues, many of the people turned away from God and to idols. In Isaiah's vision, the Lord is sitting on a lofty throne with the train of his robe filling the Temple. Seraphim attend to the Lord while two of their six wings cover their faces, two wings cover their feet, and two wings are used to fly. They call "Holy, holy, holy is the Lord of Heaven's Armies! The whole earth is filled with his glory!" The entire Temple is filled with smoke.

Isaiah proclaims "It's all over! I am doomed, for I am a sinful man. I have filthy lips, and I live among a people with filthy lips. Yet I have seen the King, the Lord of Heaven's Armies." (Isaiah 6:5). One of the seraphim flies to an altar to remove a burning coal with a pair of tongs. The seraphim then touch the burning coals to Isaiah's lips and proclaims "See, this coal has touched your lip. Now your guilt is removed, and your sins are forgiven." (Isaiah 6:6).

Isaiah's vision emphasizes God's holiness. We need to discover God's holiness in the same way that Isaiah saw God's holiness in the vision. You need to maintain a view of God as high and lifted up so that you do not forget that God has the power and ability to deal with your problems and concerns. God has the moral perfection that is necessary for our sins to be purified and our minds cleansed.

Like Isaiah, we realize our own sins separate us from God. Isaiah was forgiven after the burning coal touched his lips while we are forgiven after we ask Jesus to come into our hearts. God cleansed Isaiah just like God cleanses us. After God cleansed Isaiah, the Lord asked, "Whom should I send as a messenger to these people? Who will go for us?" Isaiah responds with "Here I am. Send me." You should be like Isaiah and volunteer to go when God shows a need.

God tells Isaiah, "Yes, go, and say to these people, 'Listen carefully, but do not understand. Watch closely, but learn nothing.' Harden the hearts of these people. Plug their ears and shut their eyes. That way, they will not see with their eyes, nor hear with their ears, nor understand with their hearts and turn to me for healing." (Isaiah 6:9-10). God had no more patience with Judah's chronic rebellion. He was going to abandon them due to their persistent rebellion and hardness of heart but wanted to ensure that the few that were open to hearing God's word had the opportunity. Isaiah's role was to be the Lord's representative to the remnant of faithful followers who would receive his mercy through the judgment. Be obedient so that you do not miss the Lord's mercy.

Isaiah asked the Lord, "Lord, how long will this go on?" The Lord's response is "Until their towns are empty, their houses are deserted, and the whole country is a wasteland; until the Lord has sent everyone away, and the entire land of Israel lies deserted. If even a tenth--a remnant-- survive, it will be invaded again and burned. But a terebinth or oak tree

leaves a stump when it is cut down, so Israel's stump will be a holy seed."
(Isaiah 6:11-13). The people who refused to listen would start listening
when they had nowhere to turn but toward God. God promised that
there would be a time when Judah would only have a small remaining
portion of each tribe on the land due to invasion. Then the people would
start to repent and listen to God. You should try to avoid being like
Judah and listen to God like the faithful remnant instead of a rebellious
majority with hardened hearts.

Chapter 3
PROPHESIES TO KING AHAZ

ISAIAH 7-12 AND ISAIAH 17

I n 734 B.C., Jerusalem was facing an impending attack from the northern kingdom of Israel and Aram. Ahaz was king of Judah and was frightened by the situation that he faced. God sent Isaiah to give a message to Ahaz. This message is Isaiah 7:1-9.

Ahaz is the son of Jotham and grandson of Uzziah. He succeeded Jotham after his death. Ahaz was a weak and idolatrous king unlike his father and grandfather who were faithful to God during their reigns. King Rezin of Syria (also known as Aram) and the kingdom of Israel formed an alliance in an attempt to attack Jerusalem but failed to carry out the plan. When the news reached the royal court of Judah of the alliance, the king and people were afraid. God instructed Isaiah to take his son Shear-jashub to meet King Ahaz at the end of the aqueduct that feeds water into the upper pool.

God's message to King Ahaz was to be careful, keep calm, and do not be afraid. Ahaz was told to not lose heart at the news of the alliance. The king of Rezin and Pekah of Israel are called burned-out embers in verse four to show that they were not a threat to Judah. God acknowledged that the kings of Syria and Israel were plotting to attack

Judah. They planned to put the son of Tabeel as the king of Judah after they won. But the Lord's message concerning the attack was this:

> This invasion will never happen; it will never take place; for Syria is no stronger than its capital, Damascus, and Damascus is no stronger than its king, Rezin. As for Israel, within sixty-five years it will be crushed and completely destroyed. Israel is no stronger than its capital, Samaria, and Samaria is no stronger than its king, Pekah, son of Remaliah. Unless your faith is firm, I cannot make you stand firm. (7:7-9, NLT)

God's warning to king Ahaz and to us is God cannot ensure that we stand firm unless our faith is firm. Part of the reason that Isaiah was instructed to take his son is because his son's name Shear-jashub means "a remnant will return". The son's presence was intended to be a reminder of God's plan for mercy and restoration after judgment.

The Sign of Immanuel

Ahaz attempted to buy aid from the Assyrians instead of standing firm in faith. Syria attacked and captured the northern kingdom of Israel. After the Lord's initial message to Ahaz, God sent a second message for King Ahaz to Isaiah. Isaiah tells Ahaz that he can ask the Lord for a sign of confirmation without limitation. God gave Ahaz no limits to what he wanted as a sign. Ahaz refused the offer with "No, I will not test the Lord like that" (Isaiah 7:12). While this might appear like Ahaz is being righteous by not wanting to test God, Ahaz was avoiding the sign of confirmation from God. We also do this by using excuses to avoid giving God our personal concerns. Then we can avoid God's answer to our concern or situation and rely on ourselves. This is often used when individuals have issues with jobs, finances, or personal relationships with the rationalization that these things are too insignificant for God's interest. God wants you to rely on him for all things including the little things.

Isaiah asks Ahaz, "Isn't it enough to exhaust human patience? Must you exhaust the patience of my God as well?" (Isaiah 7:13). God chooses the sign since Ahaz refused to do as God asked.

God chose that the sign is a virgin conceiving a child and giving birth to a son that is called Immanuel. Isaiah prophesied that Israel and Syria would be deserted within three years. Due to Ahaz's refusal to rely on God, the Lord was going to bring the king of Assyria upon Judah. The Lord would bring the army of southern Egypt and the army of Assyria to swarm around Judah. Egyptians carried off Josiah's son and Babylon, the nation that conquered Assyria, took the next king. Isaiah prophesied that when Judah would be attacked, a "razor" would be used to shave off everything (Isaiah 7:20). This is a symbol of humiliation and represents the nation being shaved of its facial hair which is a great embarrassment for a Hebrew man.

Isaiah promises that a small percentage will remain in Judah when the nation is conquered and the people are taken away from Israel. In verse twenty-one, Isaiah writes that there will be so few people that the small number of remaining livestock will provide enough milk for everyone to eat their fill of yogurt and honey. The land would not be a place of agricultural abundance but instead would become a vast expanse of briers and thorns. The fertile hillsides that the people of Isaiah's time took pride in would become grazing land for the remaining cattle, sheep, and goats.

God's punishment for the people's greed, injustice, and drunkenness was going to be taking everything they had pride in. There are times that our own sins require a similar punishment. Remember that God removes the cause of your sins to save you from destruction, He will always leave a remnant and continue to care for you.

Assyrian Invasion is Coming

Chapter eight starts with instructions from God to Isaiah that at first do not make a lot of sense. Isaiah is told to make a large signboard and write Maher-shalal-hash-baz on it. This act is witnessed by Uriah the priest and Zechariah, son of Jeberekiah. The name Maher-shalal-hash-baz means "quick to plunder, swift to the spoil". Then Isaiah received a second son and God tells him to name the son Maher-shalal-hash-baz. God continued with a warning that the king of Assyria would attack and capture both Damascus and Samaria before the boy would say his first words. Assyria captured Aram in 732 B.C. and then Assyria captured Israel in 722 B.C.

The next words from God to Isaiah concern God's actions towards Judah's rejection of God's kindness in stopping the Northern kingdom's attempt to attack Judah.

> My care for the people of Judah is like the gently flowing waters of Shiloah, but they have rejected it. They are rejoicing over what will happen to King Rezin and King Pekah. Therefore, the Lord will overwhelm them with a mighty flood from the Euphrates River--the king of Assyria and all his glory. This flood will overflow all its channels and sweep into Judah until it is chin deep. It will spread its wings, submerging your land from one end to the other, O Immanuel. (Isaiah 8:6-8)

The people of Judah rejected God's kindness and sought help from other nations instead of relying on God. The message from God shows both his love with his description of his care as gently flowing waters but also shows Gods' wrath with his promise of an attack from Assyria. His wrath is described as a submerging. When we ignore his love and guidance, we invite the same wrath. God loves us like parents love their children. He wants to protect us from bad choices but gives us the freedom to make our own choices even when they are bad. When you make those bad choices, you need to recognize the consequences of those choices instead of assuming that God will protect you from the consequences. The consequence of Judah's choice to seek help from other nations instead of relying on God was Assyria attacking them. God loves Judah but was not going to prevent Assyria from attacking like he stopped the northern kingdom from attacking.

Trust the Lord

God gave a strong warning to Isaiah not to think like everyone else. You need to consider this warning yourself and remember to not follow the ways of the current society. God should be your sanctuary and the fear that most people allow to control their lives should not control yours. Fear is a powerful enemy of faith and is a strong deterrent to a person's peace of mind. It is important to remember that the only thing that you need to fear is God. God will remove fear from your hearts if you ask for his help when you experience fear.

God instructs Isaiah and us to preserve his teaching. Previous generations preserved history through oral stories. Then it changed to preserving the writing of God's words. Later generations copied the writings onto new paper and translated it into multiple languages. Our current generation has the relatively new medium of the internet to spread the word of God. Isaiah followed God's command to preserve his teaching with his book, but you need to continue the instruction to preserve God's teaching through modern means.

While the only thing we should fear is God, we are instructed to wait for him and put our hope in him in Isaiah 8:17. This can be one of the most difficult tests for some people. Patience is not an easy behavior. Our current society praises quick service and our capacity for patience is slowly dying. God's plans usually are not quick. God did not fulfill his promise of a Messiah for seven hundred years. When you are dealing with tough situations, you need to practice patience and remember God's timing is not your timing. God has a plan to fix your tough circumstances, but they often take longer than you would prefer. While you wait, keeping hope is an important aspect that we often disregard. Without hope, you are more likely to become discouraged and fail the test.

Isaiah and his children were signs and warnings to Israel of God's plan for Israel during and after Isaiah's time. Some of the people of Isaiah's time compared him to mediums and psychics. Instead of relying on God for guidance, people were going to other sources. We often do the same things. There are still people who rely on mediums and psychics, but other idols can be used for guidance in place of God. You should look to God's instructions and teachings as said in Isaiah 8:20. Individuals who do not live according to God's teachings live in darkness. This type of life involves constant searching for meaning that causes a person to be weary, hungry, and angry. All that they can find is trouble and anguish because they are looking for peace in the wrong places. When you live by God's instructions and put your hope in him, your life has light. While you might have tests, you can keep peace of mind when you go to God for guidance.

The other lesson from Isaiah 8:21 is that the people who contradict God's word will rage and curse at their king and their God when they become weary and hungry. All they see is trouble and anguish. Then they blame God for their situation instead of accepting and recognizing that their troubles are self-induced because they refused to follow the guidance of God. Everyone will at one point rely on guidance from another source instead of God and will get into a situation mentioned in this verse. Instead of blaming God when you get into this situation, you should use the situation to find ways to grow and take steps to avoid repeating bad choices and failures.

Messiah

God does promise that the time of darkness and despair will not last forever. He meant it for Judah during their time as captives of Assyria and for us. You can feel like your troubles will never end but God will lead you safely through if you follow him wholeheartedly. This does not mean that you are spared from troubles but rather that God will ensure your safety when you follow his guidance.

Isaiah writes about where our Messiah will come from in Isaiah 9:1 when he writes that there will be a time in the future when Galilee of the Gentiles will be filled with glory. He prophesies that the northern kingdom that contains Zebulun and Naphtali would be humbled but would see a great light. This light was prophesied to come to enlarge the nation of Israel and break the yoke of slavery. Jesus is this light and grew up and ministered in the territories of Zebulun and Naphtali. Jesus broke not only the Hebrew's slavery but also our own slavery to sin. Isaiah 8:4 says:

> For you will break the yoke of their slavery and lift the heavy burden from their shoulders. You will break the oppressor's rod, just as you did when you destroyed the army of Midian.

Jesus came to deliver us from slavery to sin. This was completed with Jesus' death on the cross.

In Chapter nine, you find some of the lovely names for the Messiah that are in so many of our songs and poems. The four mentioned in verse 6 are Wonderful Counselor, Mighty God, Everlasting Father, and Prince of Peace. The promised child that is prophesied to be a son that is given to us by God will be called these names. We use these Names for Jesus. Isaiah spoke these words to the people of Judah seven hundred years before Jesus was born.

Isaiah ends this section concerning the Messiah with a description of his kingdom. He describes it as a peace that will never end. The Messiah is prophesied to rule with fairness and justice for all eternity. He will rule from the throne of his ancestor David. God gave us the Messiah because of his passionate commitment to ensure that we can come to him despite our choices that lead us away from him.

Lord's Anger against Pride

Israel and Samaria spoke with pride and arrogance against God in Isaiah's time. Pride is a common sin that lead Israel to believe that it could rebuild their nation without God. The people of Judah were putting their trust in themselves and not in God despite everything God did to provide and protect the land that they lived on. We often do the same thing. We will rely on ourselves instead of relying on God after he has given us something. God is the source of our resources and abilities and yet we take pride in our accomplishments. It is easy to forget that the reason for those accomplishments is what God has given us. Taking pride in yourself cuts you off from God because you are not relying nor looking to God for guidance.

Israel boasted that they would replace the broken bricks of the ruins with finished stone and replant the fields. Due to Israel's pride and arrogance, God promises to bring Resin's enemies against them and stir up all their foes in Isaiah 9:11. Due to God's anger at their pride, the Syrians and the Philistines were going to come into the picture and help devour Israel. This does not satisfy God's anger with his children's pride, but is intended to encourage repentance of sins. Isaiah explains that God's children do not repent nor seek the Lord after this punishment.

Due to the lack of repentance from Israel, God planned to destroy the nation in one day. He was going to destroy the leaders of Israel and the lying prophets at one time. The leaders were misleading the people and taking the nation down a path of destruction. This is not the only time that a nation has been misled by its leaders and faced punishment. We have seen this repeated over and over again throughout history with many nations. A few examples are the roman empire, Germany, and Russia.

Isaiah 9:18-20 describes wickedness and how it spreads. Wickedness does not remain isolated but quickly spreads like a forest fire. It will send up clouds of smoke as it blackens the earth due to how strongly it burns. Instead of wood being its fuel, people are the fuel for wickedness. Wickedness is so influential that it can turn people against their own family. Sadly, wickedness is endlessly hungry and never satisfied. The only way to fight wickedness is reliance on God. The northern kingdom Israel endured a civil war due to the selfishness and wickedness of the tribes of Ephraim and Manasseh which destroyed Israel. We need to fight against wickedness because of how destructive it is to families, communities, and society.

Isaiah then moves to the judgment that awaits the unjust judges of his nation. The judges were issuing unfair laws, depriving the poor of justice, and denying the rights of the needy. Instead of protecting widows and orphans, the judges were preying on the weak. Due to their actions, God was going to have them captured and taken to far away nations where they had no one to turn to for help. We can be like those unjust judges and oppress others. The punishment for oppressing others is being oppressed by others.

While God used Assyria as a weapon to express his anger, the king of Assyria did not understand his true role. God has repeated this method with nations who have rejected him in modern day. God is still in control of our world and continues to use individuals or nations that do not believe in him to punish his children who turn away from him. While the king of Assyria's plan was to destroy Judah, God's plan was to start the path of redemption for his children.

After Assyria completed what God wanted, God was going to punish them for the same sins as Israel: pride and arrogance. Assyria were proud of their military victories and bragged about their destruction of the gods of other nations. Assyria felt that no one was able to defeat them. God only viewed Assyria as a tool and was ready to discard it when it completed its purpose. A plague was sent to Assyria's proud troops. God did send Jonah to preach to them. Due to the people's reaction to Jonah's preaching, Assyria's punishment was delayed. Assyria was never able to capture Judah and was destroyed by Babylon in 612 B.C. The city was completely destroyed and was buried until the nineteenth century. This fulfills Isaiah 10 where it is written that it would be consumed by fire and so few would survive that a child could count them.

Hope for the Remnant

After Judah was to be captured, a remnant was going to remain in Israel but there would be so few that there would be no issues with resources in the destroyed land. The few remaining people would faithfully trust the Lord instead of allies. The important quality of the remnant would be their faith in God. Isaiah promised that Assyria would be stopped at the city of Nob when they marched toward Jerusalem. The city of Nob is only two miles from Jerusalem, but Assyria never entered the city of Jerusalem as God promised.

The Messiah

The Messiah was prophesied to come from David's Line in Isaiah 11:1. The Messiah was given the Spirit of the Lord which included the Spirit of wisdom and understanding, Spirit of counsel and might, Spirit of knowledge, and fear of the Lord. Unlike us, the Messiah naturally delights in obeying the Lord, not judging by appearance, nor making unfair judgments. You can train your hearts to follow the Messiah's example and act fairly toward others. One of the primary purposes of the Messiah was to restore justice to the poor due the corruption level in Judah. The nation needed a revival of righteousness, justice, and faithfulness. Our own society has reached a similar state. Society rewards selfishness and greed instead of helping those in need. The Messiah wears righteousness like a belt and truth like an undergarment. We all need to follow the Messiah's example and work on living our lives with righteousness and truth to fight the selfishness and greed in our society.

A time of peace is prophesied that will be brought by Christ's second coming. This time of peace is described in Isaiah 11:6-10. It will be a golden age when prey and predator will live together with children able to lead the animals and play safely nearby. Isaiah 11:9 states that nothing will hurt or destroy in all my holy mountain, for as the waters fill the sea, so the earth will be filled with people who know the Lord. During this golden age, the Messiah will be a banner of salvation to all the world. Nature will return to its intended balance and harmony along with perfect tranquility when Christ returns to reign over the earth.

The Messiah will bring back the remnant of his people for a second time from those of his people that remain in all distant lands. He will assemble the exiles of Israel and gather the people of Judah. God will provide a way for his people to return when the Messiah returns. We have seen God use other nations to assist the people of Judah to return to Israel after World War II. The last verse of chapter eleven tells us that God will make a highway for his people. We do not know what pathway he will provide us. He promised that we will be able to reach the Messiah when the time arrives just as God provided a way for the Israelites to return home from Assyria and Egypt.

A Hymns of Praise

Isaiah 12

> I will praise you, O Lord!
> You were angry with me, but not any more.
> Now you comfort me.
> See, God has come to save me.
> I will trust in him and not be afraid.
> The Lord God is my strength and my song;
> He has given me victory.
>
> Thank the Lord! Praise his name!
> Tell the nations what he has done.
> Let them know how mighty he is!
> Sing to the Lord, for he has done wonderful things.
> Make known his praise around the world.
> Let all the people of Jerusalem shout his praise with joy!
> For great is the Holy One of Israel who lives among you.

These are two different hymns of praise that Isaiah says will be sung on the day that the Messiah returns. These hymns show the joy that we will have on that day. The hymns include expressions of gratitude, praises, and promises to spread knowledge about our Lord. These are all things that we should be doing now and not just when he returns to us. You should have your life demonstrate the words of these hymns by thanking God, praising him, and spreading the word about him. As Isaiah 12:2b states the Lord God is my strength and my song; he has given me victory.

Damascus

The seventeenth chapter of Isaiah finishes the prophecies first mentioned in chapter seven. At the time that Isaiah spoke this message, Judah was in an alliance with Damascus and was paying tribute to Tiglathpileser III. Yet Isaiah warns the people that the city of Damascus would completely disappear and would become a heap of ruins. Due to Israel's alliance with the city, Israel would have a similar fate and its fortified town would be destroyed.

Isaiah informed the king and the people that Israel's glory would become dim and its body would waste away. It was a desolate picture of no crops and empty fields in verses five and six. The reason for this extreme decision from God was due to Aram's decision to turn from God. They decided to depend on idols and their own strength instead. We can fall into the same trap and depend on the idols of our times and our successes instead of looking to God. You reap grief and pain when you fail to learn from their mistakes. Eternal security comes from God alone. Trust in God not in the false allurements of temporal things around us.

After this grief and pain fell upon Damascus, Syria, and Israel; the people of Judah did look to their creator instead of relying on the idols that came to them from other countries such as Canaan. It took God making Israel's cities abandoned and desolate. God's people at the time did not use God in the way he intended. Isaiah 17:10 explains how God meant for us to see him. He is to be our Rock that can hide us so that we can plant the finest grapevines. We would best understand it today as God wanting to be our shield to protect us so that we can plant the seed of his word for society. If we do not use God as our Rock, then our fruit will be grief and unrelieved pain.

There is some happy news in chapter seventeen. The last three verses (12-14) show a vision of Assyria being overthrown. Many nations would come together to defeat the nation. God would be the one to silence them and force them to flee. Assyria would be destroyed for its role in plundering and destroying Israel. Even though God punished his children for their sins, He also provided a fitting end for those who had a role in their punishment.

The best thing that we can take out of these chapters is that we should learn from the decision that the people of Isaiah's time made and turn from our own idols to God. You will not always turn to God in times of trouble, but God will always have a path back to prosperity ready for those who turn to him as their rock.

Chapter 4

PROPHESIES TO KING HEZEKIAH

ISAIAH 13-16, 18-23

When Ahaz died in 726 B.C., his son Hezekiah became king. Hezekiah's name means "God has strengthened." He was unlike his father and was faithful to God. Isaiah had spent years prophesying to King Ahaz and continued to do so with Hezekiah. Judah was disorganized and owed a large tribute to Assyria for protection. Hezekiah brought about a time of great reformation during his reign. Idols were destroyed, the temple was reopened and cleansed, and worship of God was restored. Due to his trust in God, he prospered and was able to gain independence from Assyria. Isaiah was his trusted adviser. There were times of trouble, Hezekiah did make some mistakes such as paying tribute to Sennacherib and showing the wealth of Jerusalem to envoys from Babylon. Despite Hezekiah's mistakes, God provided great prestige and power to Hezekiah during his reign due to the trust that Hezekiah had in God.

Isaiah did provide some messages to Hezekiah during his reign concerning other nations that are included in the book of Isaiah. These chapters contain messages concerning Babylon, Assyria, and Moab.

Babylon

When Isaiah gave this message, Assyria was still the dominant power of the world and Babylon was under Assyria's control. In 605 B.C., Babylon became the dominant world power. It remained in control until 539 when Medes and Persia destroyed Babylon. This is Isaiah's first message of judgment on other nations. Isaiah continues this message in the last three verses of chapter 12: God would punish their greatest enemies.

The Lord was going to raise an army against Babylon to express his anger toward Babylon. The army would destroy the whole land of Babylon. Isaiah 13:11 states that "I, the Lord will punish the world for its evil and the wicked for their sin. I will crush the arrogance of the proud and humble the pride of the mighty." Babylon had not conquered Judah when Isaiah made this statement. This statement does not apply only to Babylon. God still punishes the world for its evil and the wicked for their sins.

Isaiah provided specific details of Babylon's destruction such as mentioning Medes being one of the countries that would be used to destroy them. No compassion was going to be shown to the Babylonians during the days of destruction. While Babylon would be described as the most glorious of kingdoms and the flower of Chaldean pride at some point after Isaiah's death, its reign would not last. God would destroy them like he destroyed Sodom and Gomorrah. Furthermore, Isaiah properly prophesied that Babylon would never be inhabited again. It has remained empty for generation after generation as Isaiah says in Isaiah 13:20. A hundred years before Babylon was going to become a dominant world power, Isaiah informed Hezekiah that Babylon's days were numbered and that its destruction was coming.

Isaiah did promise that the Lord would have mercy on the descendants of Jacob in Isaiah 14:1. Israel would be chosen as God's special people and brought back to their own land. It would not only be the Israelites coming, but people from many different nations are prophesied to join them and unite with the people of Israel.

Isaiah promised that there was going to be a day after the people returned that they would taunt the king of Babylon. This would occur on a wonderful day when the people would have no sorrow or fear. The Lord would destroy Babylon and its people because it tried to be above God. We need to learn from the mistakes that Babylon and its people made by placing their confidence in human power instead of God. Human power fades but God's power is eternal.

Babylon bragged about its ability to defeat God. Isaiah 14:13 and 14 provides Babylon's previous statements concerning their power. Babylon promised to ascend to heaven and set its throne above God's stars. Then they thought that they would preside on the mountain of the gods and be like the Most High. God promises that Babylon would be taken down to the place of the dead. Lord promised in Isaiah 22-23 that he would rise against Babylon and would destroy it. He was going to make it a desolate place instead of allowing it to prosper.

Assyria

Then Isaiah moves to God's plans for Assyria in Isaiah 14:24-27. God promised to break the Assyrians and ensure that Israel would no longer be their slaves. It is short and sweet. The main point is stated in verse 26 with Isaiah's statement from God: "I have a plan for the whole earth, a hand of judgment upon all the nations." God continues to have a plan for the whole earth.

Philistia

Chapter fourteen ends with a message for the Philistines. God tells the Philistines to not rejoice at the death of the king of Assyria who had previously attacked Philistia. There was a threat coming that was even more dangerous. After a powerful army, a famine was going to come and destroy the remaining few. God promises that Jerusalem would be a refuge to God's oppressed people.

Moab

Chapter 15 and 16 provide God's plan to punish Moab for its treatment of Israel. He starts with plans to level the town of Ar and destroy the city of Kir. These cities were attacked by Assyria several times in 700 B.C. The people would mourn the loss of loved ones and homes. Other cities would face similar outcomes and are mentioned in these chapters. Nebo and Medeba would wail while Heshbon and Elealeh would cry out. The nation would be helpless with fear.

God's heart would weep for Moab. It is the descendants of Lot. Its people would flee with their possession in an attempt to run from its aggressor. A tribute of lambs from Sela would be sent to Israel in an attempt to seek refuge in Israel by some of the remaining Moabs. The women of Moab would ask for help. Isaiah did advise that Judah accept the refugees and show them compassion.

The Moab would face oppression and destruction because of its pride, arrogance, and rage. The nation would mourn due to its past actions. Moab rebelled against God and ignored him due to their pride. Moabites worshiped at pagan shrines instead of worshiping God. Farms and vineyards would no longer be fruitful and no shouts of joy would be heard at the harvest.

We are often like the Moabites and seek our own ways to solve our troubles instead of relying on God. The Moabites turned to idols and pagan gods instead of God. We often turn toward more modern things before turning to God in our times of trouble. Do the opposite of the Moabites, turn to God and not idols.

This was not the first time that God had predicted Moab's outcome. Isaiah promised that God's plans for Moab would occur within three years and the glory of Moab would come to an end with only a few of its people remaining.

Messiah

In Isaiah 16:4-5, God promises to establish one of David's descendants as king after the oppression and destruction in Moab have ended. This king would rule with mercy and truth.

King Hezekiah's reign

These are the prophecies that are known to be given to King Hezekiah early in his reign. King Hezekiah was unlike his father and rallied the people to repent so that God would not send them into exile like the northern kingdom of Israel had been. King Hezekiah did many good things for the nations such as reopening the Temple, orchestrating a national celebration of Passover, and reforming the religious practices. The most important thing that he did was order the people to destroy the idols that were being worshiped during King Ahaz's reign. Hezekiah reigned for 29 years and his actions were mostly pleasing and good for God which led to a spiritual renewal in Judah.

Isaiah did continue to prophesy to King Hezekiah and the people of Judah. The next messages were given between 714 B.C. and 701 B.C. These messages are from Isaiah for other nations. While the messages are about nations that Judah interacted with for foreign affairs, they do include advice to the kingdom of Judah on how to deal with them that we can use to guide our own interaction with the secular world.

Ethiopia

Isaiah called Ethiopia a land of fluttering sails that lies at the headwaters of the Nile in Isaiah 18:1. Ethiopia was a target of Assyria and was seeking help from surrounding nations including Judah. Isaiah advised King Hezekiah to not respond to the ambassadors and rely on God. The Lord had a plan for Assyria. Ethiopia's plan of an alliance to defeat Assyria was not God's plan. The Lord told Isaiah that "I will watch quietly from my dwelling place—as quietly as the heat rises on a summer day, or as the morning dew forms during the harvest" (Isaiah 18:4) concerning Ethiopia's plan.

Egypt

King Hezekiah was considering an alliance with Egypt against Assyria. Isaiah warned Hezekiah and the people of Judah against the formation of an alliance. He prophesied that Assyria would be destroyed in God's time. Isaiah was reminding the people to hold on to hope and remember that God's plan was going to happen in God's time. Making plans with other nations was not going to hasten the time.

Isaiah informed the people of Judah that God was going to cause a civil war in Egypt that would have brother fighting brother. Egypt would plead with their idols, but God would hand Egypt over to a fierce king (Isaiah 19: 2-4). Additionally, God was going to prevent the flooding that Egypt's land needed for a good crop and cause the fish to leave. God especially focuses his attention on the wise counselors of the pharaoh who boasted of their wisdom. In verse fourteen, Isaiah tells the people that the Lord has sent a spirit of foolishness on the officials of Zoan so that all their suggestions were wrong and leading Egypt astray. Egypt would become weak and would cower in fear.

Isaiah makes a few prophesizes of what Egypt will do on the day when Christ comes to reign starting in Isaiah 19:19. There will be an altar to the Lord in the heart of Egypt, a monument to the Lord at its border, and a highway between Egypt and Assyria. The Egyptians will turn to the Lord and way from their idols just like Assyria.

On the day that Christ reigns, former enemies will be united in love. Christ breaks down all barriers including the ones that threaten relationships. We need to remember this message in our daily lives. While we might feel like there is no way to connect with another individual, there is no barrier that the Lord cannot remove. Jesus is available to all and you just need to show God's love through your actions and be an example of his love through kindness.

Egypt has a bad history with Israel and Assyria but that does not matter in God's final plan. When Christ returns, Egypt, Assyria, and Israel will all unite in worship to God. All will be blessed. It does not matter if you received salvation as a child or as an adult, if you pray and receive Christ saving power. All who turn to Christ will worship and be blessed on that day.

Symbol of Terrible Troubles

Isaiah 20 occurred in 711 B.C. when Sargon II was king of Assyria. Sargon sent his commander in chief to capture Ashdod, a Philistine city. In response, God instructed Isaiah to take off his clothes and sandals and walk around naked and barefoot. After over three years of following God's instructions, the Lord had Isaiah explain why he had Isaiah do it. It was a symbol of terrible troubles that would fall on Egypt and Ethiopia. It was a humiliating experience for Isaiah to do as God commanded. The same kind of humiliation would fall on Egypt and Ethiopia. Israel was considering entering an alliance with these countries at this time. The message to Judah was "Do not put your trust in foreign governments".

God was going to have the king of Assyria attack Egypt and Ethiopia and take prisoners. The prisoners would be made to walk naked and barefoot like Isaiah did. If Judah did enter an alliance with these nations and rely on Egypt to protect them from Assyria, then Judah would reap the consequences of relying on something other than God. We tend to do the same thing that Judah was considering. We look to alliances with human sources instead of relying on God when we see trouble coming. Some of the institutions that we consider for alliances are the government, science, education, medical care, and financial systems. While we do not consciously put our hope in these institutions, we often look to either legislation, technology, higher education, medical services, or financial resources to fix a situation before looking to God. While it is not wrong to use resources available, you need to purposely look to God first and rely on him instead of the world around you.

Babylon, Edom, Arabia

Isaiah 21 goes from talking about Egypt to giving a prophecy concerning Babylon and other nations. Isaiah foretold that disaster was going to befall Babylon. Babylon was going to be attacked. This was either fulfilled in 700 B.C. when Babylon revolted against Assyria or in 539 B.C. when Babylon fell.

In Isaiah 21:6, the Lord tells Isaiah to put a watchman on the city wall to look for chariots and be fully alert. This was meant as a sign of destruction coming and for Judah to be on the look out for trouble. Isaiah continues to prophecy that one day the watchman would call out and announce the appearance of a chariot with a pair of horses. The watchman would need to announce that Babylon had fallen. Babylon was a powerful city that was filled with horrible sin. The destruction of Babylon was a sign of how idols do not protect against the will of God because Babylon was a symbol of all that stood against God.

This process of destroying Babylon was part of God's threshing and winnowing the earth. God was breaking open the seed and then throwing them in the air so that the worthless chaff would blow away and the good grain would be left. God was removing the sinful, rebellious people with the destruction of Babylon while keeping the followers of God.

Verse eleven through twelve of the chapter moves over to God's plan for Edom. Edom was a constant enemy of Israel. Edom was created from the descendants of Esau. Edom consistently rejoiced at Judah's downfall and was destroyed for their part in wanting Judah to fall.

Chapter 21 ends with a message concerning Arabia. The verses mention Dedan, Tema, and Kedar. They were border cities in Arabia that controlled the trade routes. God warns Isaiah that the refugees would need to hide in the deserts. Judah was told to help the few refugees that would survive.

Jerusalem

The first part of Isaiah 22 is a message from God concerning Jerusalem—the Valley of Vision. This message was an attempt to get God's people to return to him. If Judah did not return to God, then the message warns that Jerusalem would be attacked due to the trust in their own ingenuity, their weapons, and other nations. Jerusalem would have bodies killed by famine and disease with leaders fleeing and surrendering without resistance due to their decision to not rely on God.

Isaiah mourned in Isaiah 21:4 and wept for his people being destroyed because they would not repent and choose God's judgment. We often act like the people of Judah and choose to rely on other things instead of God. We often choose God's judgment instead of repentance like the people of Judah did during Isaiah's time.

The walls of Jerusalem would be broken when Assyria attacked with all its vassals including Elam and Kir. When Assyria approached to attack, Jerusalem would fall if Judah relied on their own work instead of asking for help from God. Instead of seeking God, Judah got their weapons, inspected and strengthened the walls, and reserved their water in preparation. Isaiah 21:12 tells Judah to shave their heads in sorrow for their sins and wear clothes of burlap to show their remorse. Yet Judah would feast and drink when Assyria surrounded them because they gave up hope and still refused to repent and turn to God. Judah did not trust God's power to save them from their circumstance. This is the reason that God allowed Jerusalem to be attacked so that his people would return to him.

We still see people living without hope which results in despair or self-indulgence. We continue to not seek God and either self-indulge like the people of Judah or throw a pity party. Turn to God and his promises when you are surrounded by trouble. In times of trouble, your first response should be to trust in God and turn to him.

Shebna

The last portion of Isaiah 22 is a message to Judah concerning Shebna. The Lord told Isaiah that Judah should confront Shebna, the palace administrator. The message to Shebna was to make him and the rest of Judah realize how materialistic they were. Shebna was building a beautiful tomb for himself as an example of his materialism. Due to his decision to put his faith in things, God was going to drive him out of office and have Eliakim replace him as palace administrator. The palace administrator was the highest position in the royal court and had a lot of respect and honor. It was a highly sought after position and it was a great dishonor to lose it. Even Eliakim, who would serve God and bring honor to his family, would fail because the kingdom of Judah would choose to rely on themselves, possessions, and alliances instead of God.

Tyre

Isaiah 23 gives the last prophecy to King Hezekiah concerning another nation. Tyre was a famous city of the ancient world that was a major trading center due to its large seaport. The city was very wealthy and very evil. Isaiah is not the only prophet to rebuke Tyre and Judah's association with it. The Lord has Isaiah give another warning against political alliances with unstable neighbors.

The Lord informs Isaiah that Tyre would be gone and its destruction would cause great sorrow by the nations, specifically Egypt, due to its position as a trading center and seaport. The Lord was causing the destruction of Tyre because princes and nobles relied on Tyre for security instead of God. Verse 23:9 states that "The Lord of Heaven's Armies has done it to destroy your pride and bring low all earth's nobility." The Lord hates our pride because it separates us from him. The destruction of Tyre was necessary because of the pride of the princes and nobles. God will sometimes destroy something that causes you to have pride to remind you to turn to him. The destruction of Tyre is an example of this.

Even though the Lord was going to have Tarshish destroy Tyre, it would not be forgotten forever. The city would be forgotten for seventy years and then return to life. The city did return to life after the Israelites returned from their captivity in Babylon. The Israelites traded with Tyre when they returned from captivity. The city of Tyre was no different when it returned to life and was once again a trading center for other nations to use.

Chapter 5

FINAL PROPHECIES BEFORE ASSYRIAN'S ATTACK

ISAIAH 24-27, 29-35

T hese are the last prophecies that Isaiah gave before the Assyrian attack. Isaiah 24-27 are sometimes called Isaiah's Apocalypse because they focus on God's judgment on the entire world. The chapters describe the last days and are similar to Revelations because they describe the last days when God will judge the whole world.

Destruction of the Earth

Chapter 24 starts with the prophecy of the Lord destroying the earth. God is going to destroy the earth and turn it into a vast wasteland in the final days. Everyone will be scattered. The earth suffers the effects of human evil and lawbreaking. It will mourn and dry up in the final days. Everyone will waste away. Pollution, crime, addiction, and poverty are examples of how human sin affects the earth. Everyone is affected by sin including believers. Due to human's sin and its effect on the Earth, a curse consumes the earth. Humankind will be destroyed by fire to pay for the price of their sin.

Isaiah 24:7-13 describes a sad and dismal scene of what will be left after the fire consumes the earth. There will be no grapes to create wine, no celebrations with music, and cities will be in chaos and ruins. Instead of joy and gladness, there will be gloom and mourning. Only a remnant of humankind will remain during this time.

The remnant of believers will shout and sing for joy in demonstration of God's righteousness. The remnant will hold onto God's promises for the future and praise him. We need to be like the remnant and sing his praises instead of letting the world's condition make us depressed. Isaiah describes a world that is much like ours. A world where deceit prevails, treachery is everywhere, and terror and traps are rampant. Destruction continues to occur and the earth foundations shake. The earth is heading in a path of destruction and will fall due to the guilt of rebellion.

In the final days, Good will punish all the spiritual forces that oppose God and the proud rulers of the nations. After God punishes the gods of others and the rulers, the moon will wane, and the sun will fade. Then the Lord will rule in Jerusalem.

Praise for Judgment and Salvation

This is Isaiah's words to God in an expression of honor and praise for the Lord. Isaiah appreciates the Lord keeping his promise and doing as he planned to eternally save us. God fulfilled his promises to the people of Judah just like he fulfills his promises to us. We need to remember to praise him for his goodness and faithfulness instead of focusing on the troubles to come. While the prophecy of the destruction of the Earth is scary, it was all planned a long time ago by God so that we could join him in a place without sin.

Even in times of troubles, we need to remember what Isaiah says in Isaiah 25:4 that the Lord is a tower of refuge to the poor and needy. He is a refuge from the storm and a shelter from the heat. Ruthless people oppress the poor and seek to make others' lives harder. When you are being oppressed, you need to turn to God for comfort and help because he is your refuge.

The Lord will silence the foreign nations and stop the boasting of the ruthless people. The Lord will spread a wonderful feast for gentiles and Jews that will be a delicious banquet to celebrate the overthrowing of evil. The cloud of gloom and shadow of death will be removed during that feast. These believers at the feast will see God finish his plan to save us from death. The Lord will wipe away all tears, remove all insults, and mockery. The people at the feast will proclaim God and rejoice because of his plan for salvation. All who oppose God and rebel against him will be crushed while He protects those who follow him. The destruction of the Earth will end the pride and evil works of people who oppose him. While it will not be an easy time, it will complete God's plan so that you can be with him and not be separated by your sins.

A Song of Praise to the Lord

Chapter 26 continues to the Song of praise that everyone will sing in Judah during that feast when God establishes his kingdom. It is a psalm of trust, praise, and meditation. It begins with acknowledging that you are surrounded by the walls of God's salvation and the gates will open to all who are righteous so that the faithful can enter.

While you are not able to completely avoid strife, you can know perfect peace by putting your trust in God and fixing your thoughts on him instead of the world around you. God's love and power will support and protect you while you go through troubles. He provides you the peace that the world is unable to provide. While God provides peace to those who focus on him, he humbles the proud and arrogant.

When you do not focus your thoughts on him and instead focus on your accomplishments, you risk His judgment.

In verse seven, Isaiah states that "for those who are righteous, the way is not steep and rough, you are a God who does what is right, and you smooth out the path ahead of them." While life may not always seem smooth, God is there to aid, comfort, and lead you. He provides aid by giving you a purpose for your actions. God also provides the provisions you need to accomplish His goals which include relationships. God has also given you wisdom to make decisions and the ability to trust in him for comfort. You can show your trust in God by obeying his laws and glorifying his name.

A big lesson that we need to keep in mind from Isaiah 26:10 is that "Although others do right, the wicked keep doing wrong and take no notice of the Lord's majesty." Even God's followers sometimes need God's judgment to teach us before we can receive God's gifts. The wicked do benefit in our world and sometimes it is because of the forgiveness and grace that Christians give in the name of God. While we would love to see our kindness lead the wicked to changing their ways, that is not always going to happen. It is common for the wicked to keep doing wrong. Do not pay attention to the actions of others, but instead focus on God and remain eager to defend God's people.

Verses 12 through 15 of Isaiah 26 is all about praising God for what he has done for us and through us. All we accomplish is from him and he makes our nations great. For these actions, you need to worship only him and give him glory. It is a reminder to keep your focus on him since all things come from him.

The Psalm ends with a few verses about the pain of being separated from him but contains an assurance that we will be reconnect with him. We search for him when we are in distress and our prayers seek aid. While we will suffer pain and agony on the earth due to the separation from God, death is not the end if we believe in the Lord. Our bodies will rise again if we keep our trust in him. God will provide life-giving light to his people after death. This promise of everlasting life after death needs to be remembered in times of trouble because our time on earth is short but our life with God after death is everlasting.

Restoration for Israel

The last verse of Isaiah 26 is a vision of when God returns to the earth to judge it. Isaiah warns the people to go home, lock their doors, and hide themselves until the Lord's anger has passed. When the Lord comes from Heaven, he will punish people for their sins. At this point, hiding will no longer be an option for those who do not believe. Remember that there is no hiding our sins from God on that day nor now. You need to confess your sins and seek forgiveness instead of hiding your sinful thoughts and actions from God while we wait for him to return.

Isaiah 27 continues with a description of what to expect when God returns to Earth. The Lord will conquer evil on that day. Evil is described as a monster that is the enemy of God's created order. Evil will be crushed and abolished. Then God will work on restoring the vineyard for his people. He will watch over the vineyard, water it, and protect it from harm. Then the vineyard will be fruitful again and will influence the whole earth.

The Lord exiled Israel to purge the wickedness that has gained a hold of the nation. While some would say God was punishing them, he was purifying them so that all her sins could be removed. We sometimes act like Israel when God is trying to purify us. We ask why he is punishing us and do not see that he is trying to remove our sins. Israel's spiritual life was like dead branches of a tree. God was providing the strength for a living faith, but the people of Israel had turned away from God and were not receiving it. This caused the spiritual life of Israel to dry up and die which made them useless for God's plans. We often act the same way and will turn from God instead of accepting his strength. God shows no pity or mercy to those who turn from him (Isaiah 27:11).

The Lord will gather all his people together to worship the Lord on his holy mountain. The people will be from all over the earth. While Isaiah does not go into a lot of detail, we will be gathered when God is ready.

A Message about Jerusalem

Isaiah 29 starts with a warning for Jerusalem in "What sorrow awaits Ariel, the City of David." Ariel is a special name for Jerusalem with the possible meaning of "lion of god" or "altar hearth". Disaster was coming towards Jerusalem even though the people continued to celebrate the feasts each year. The city was going to be like its name and become an altar covered with blood.

God was going to become the city's enemy and destroy the city. He would crush the human enemies and drive away the attackers afterwards. God would act for Jerusalem with thunder, earthquake, and great noise to remove the enemies attacking Mount Zion. The Lord gave a spirit of deep sleep to the people of Judah which caused them to be blind, unwise, and staggering. The prophets' and visionaries' eyes were closed by God which meant that the vision given to Isaiah was not able to be seen by the other prophets.

The Lord told Isaiah in Isaiah 29:13:

> These people say they are mine.
> They honor me with their lips, but
> their hearts are far from me.
> And their worship of me is nothing but man-
> made rules learned by rote.

We can often be like the people of Judah and claim to be close to God but are disobedient and go through the motions without really having faith in God. The Greek version says that their worship is a farce. We can do the same thing and worship with our lips and not our hearts.

Lord continues in verse 14:

> Because of this, I will once again astound these
> hypocrites with amazing wonders.
> The wisdom of the wise will pass away, and the
> intelligence of the intelligent will disappear.

God was going to bring judgment due to Israel's hypocrisy. The people's worship had become routine instead of real, which is a habit that we can get into ourselves. Everyone is capable of this hypocrisy. When you start to slip into habits of worship without giving love and devotion during worship, you are being hypocritical. The purpose of worship is meant to give love and glory to God and not supposed to be lip service. Our worship needs to be honest and sincere. When it is not, we are like Judah in Isaiah and are being disobedient to God.

The people in Judah were acting like God was blind to their evil deeds and plans. The people were trying to hide their plans from God. Isaiah is blunt to them and asks in Isaiah 29:16 "How foolish can you be? He is the Potter, and he is certainly greater than you, the clay!" We can start thinking the same thoughts and act like the people in Judah. God is our father, but unlike our earthly parents, He is all knowing. There is no hiding your deeds and plans from him.

Isaiah 29 ends with a promise of better times for his people. Isaiah tells of God's promise of what life will be like when Christ rules. The land will be fertile with bountiful crops. The deaf will hear and the blind will see. Violence and gloom will be gone, and the world will be filled with joy and fairness to everyone. We will no longer have shame and will gain understanding that we cannot gain here on the earth. It is going to be a wonderful place where we have no fear of the dangers that we face here.

Judah's Worthless Treaty with Egypt

The first seven verses of Isaiah 30 are a warning to the people of Judah concerning the treaty with Egypt. It starts with God's warning of "What sorrow awaits my rebellious children." The people of Judah were being rebellious against God and were negotiating with Egypt for an alliance instead of relying on God. God continues with "You make plans that are contrary to mine. You make alliances not directed by my Spirit, thus piling up your sins." The alliance with Egypt was not in God's plan for Judah. Instead of consulting God, King Hezekiah sought an alliance with Egypt. The king and the people of Judah were placing their trust in Pharaoh's protection instead of trusting God to protect them.

We can do the same thing and put our trust in a job, a country, other people, or money instead of in God. Instead of consulting God in times of trouble, we look to worldly items for protection and comfort. Isaiah warned the people that all who depended on Pharaoh would be shamed and disgraced. Hezekiah was sending bribes to Egypt to pay for protection, yet God warns that Egypt would give nothing to Judah. This section ends with the words that Egypt's promises are worthless. The promise of security and protection from our modern-day idols is just as worthless.

Rebellious Judah

Chapter 30 then goes to a message of warning for Judah. God tells Isaiah that the people were stubborn rebels who refused to pay attention to the Lord's instruction in verse nine. The people of Judah sought good news and did not want to accept the truth that God was trying to tell them. We often will do the same when the truth makes us uncomfortable like it made the people of Judah. We prefer lies and illusions of security instead of facing reality. Face reality instead of believing in lies that make you temporarily feel better.

The Lord's response to Judah's rebellion starts in verse twelve. Judah decided to trust in oppression and lies instead of on God. Calamity was going to be the outcome of Judah's rebellion which was going to shatter them. God warns the people that they must return to God and rely on his strength. While relying on God requires patience and strength, you can avoid the mistakes of Judah and allow God to act. God wants to be your strength in difficult and good times. .

Blessings for the Lord's People

Chapter 30 ends with a message of blessing for his people. God is faithful and is waiting for his people to come to him so that he can show his love and compassion. Blessed are those who wait for God's help. God will respond to the sounds of Jerusalem's weeps and give them help when they ask.

Even in times of adversity, God is with us. As Isaiah says in verse 20, "Though the Lord gave you adversity for food and suffering for drink, he will still be with you to teach you. You will see your teacher with your own eyes." We will face adversity and suffering but God promises to be with us, teach us, and guide us during hard times. We grow through our adversity and should not look on them negatively but as the teaching tool that God intends them to be. God corrected the people of Judah when they left his path, but the people had to be willing to follow his voice. Your heart can hear his voice, but you must be willing to follow his directions.

God promised to bless the people with rain for a good harvest after they destroyed all idols. God will heal his people and provide a brighter moon and sun for his people. He is going to come back to us for Judgment. God will be burning with anger and filled with fury when he comes to pass judgment on the earth. He will be surrounded by thick, rising smoke and his words will consume like fire. God's judgment is for those who rebel against his ways, but he will bless those who are faithful to him. The proud will be led to destruction and ruin.

While God promises to guide and bless those who listen to him and are faithful, God does promise judgment for those that oppose him. God's judgment is not going to be pleasant and will end in ruin for those who do not have faith. The people of God will be filled with joy when God shows himself. God will show himself with a majestic voice, a mighty arm, and a devouring flame. God promised to strike down the Assyrians for the people of Judah. God can and will destroy our enemies like he destroyed the Assyrians. It usually will not occur as you plan but God will provide a way to destroy your enemies.

Futility of Alliances

Isaiah reiterates his position concerning Judah's choice to rely on Egypt instead of God in chapter 31. The first verse of chapter 31 is a good summary of Isaiah's position:

- What sorrow awaits those who look to Egypt for help, trusting their horses, chariots, and charioteers and depending on the strength of human armies instead of looking to the Lord, the Holy One of Israel. Isaiah 31:1

Judah looked to other nations for military help instead of looking to God. The people were trusting in human beings instead of God. We have the same tendency and often will look toward human beings for help in matters before looking toward God. We often have the same motives that the people of Judah had when they turned to Egypt instead of God: serving their own interests and not wanting to pay God's price.

Judah was more interested in their own self-interests than in God's interest. Due to their desire to focus on their own interest, the king and the people of Judah did not even consult God and instead immediately looked to human sources of help. Part of the reason the people of Judah and ourselves do not go to God for help is that we know that we do not want to pay the price necessary to obtain God's help. It means repenting of our sinful ways which is a step that the people of Judah did not want to do. We are often the same way and will look to human sources instead of God because we want to avoid the things that God wants us to do.

Isaiah is clear that God would send a great disaster that the people of Judah would not be able to avoid due to their choice. The people of Judah looked to Egypt and its military power as a type of idol. Even though Judah did not look to God for protection, God was still going to protect Jerusalem and defend it. It was not because the people deserved it, the people of Judah were being wicked rebels, but because God knew that his people would return to him. The people of Judah had to turn from their gold idols and silver images, while we must turn from money, fame, and success. Our modern idols are not as tangible, but they still take our time, energy, and devotion away from God. They are a source that cannot provide the salvation and protection that God can.

God promised that he would destroy the Assyrians. God was going to have them taken as captives. God wanted to show the people of Judah that they should look to him and not humans. We still need this lesson in modern days because we are like the people of Judah that Isaiah was speaking to. It is futile to think that human sources will win over God, but we continue to make this mistake. Next time you have a choice between God and a human source for protection, seek God's will and not your own self-interest.

Israel's Ultimate Deliverance

Chapter 32 goes to the promise of Jesus Christ who provides the ultimate deliverance. Jesus Christ is the righteous king that Isaiah prophecies is coming. The people of Judah had endured evil kings who had created much injustice for the people. This had created a strong desire for a strong king that would rule with justice. We see the same situation in our current society where a strong desire for justice is sought by the people. Jesus Christ was the answer to the people in Isaiah's time and our own time. Jesus will reign in righteousness and rule with justice one day.

Isaiah promises that a righteous king is coming who will have honest princes ruling under him. The princes will be honest, understanding, and full of sense. When this time arrives, people's motives will be transparent so that fools will not be seen as heroes and scoundrels will lose respect. Deception will be impossible to maintain so that individuals who oppose God's standard of living will be unable to hide their true position with God. It will be a time that will separate the children of God who oppose sin from the individuals who want to sin but appear good.

The people of Jerusalem were smug in false security and instead of being alert for trouble, they were lying around in ease and enjoying their current wealth and luxury. Isaiah promised that in a little more than a year's time, Jerusalem would have failing crops which would ensure that the people would have to start caring. Isaiah's warning was an attempt to get the people in Jerusalem to get out of their complacency and look to God before disaster struck their land and homes. We can fall into the same trap as the people of Jerusalem did and be lulled into a false sense of security with wealth and luxury. It is important that you remember to look to God's purpose for your life. When you abandon God's help, disaster comes if you are not doing God's purpose.

God is going to pour the Spirit on his people from Heaven in the time of Ultimate Deliverance so that the wilderness would become a fertile field that could yield bountiful crops. This is the way that God changes people's conditions here on earth. True peace and fruitfulness can be achieved with God's Spirit among us. Justice will rule in the wilderness when God establishes his kingdom for all eternity and righteousness will bring peace. God's Spirit will be fully poured on us in the future, but you can experience God's Spirit today which brings peace with it.

When God establishes his kingdom for his children, it will be a place filled with security and quiet that will allow us to rest. God promises to bless his people even though there will be times of trouble in your lives. It is important that you remember the big picture. You are loved and cared for by God even when the small picture only contains trouble.

Assyria

Assyria was a country that Judah had to deal with during Isaiah's time. It demanded other nations to keep promises but continually broke their own promises to other nations not to destroy them. Assyria betrayed and destroyed without being betrayed back. God promised that Assyria would be destroyed when it was done destroying and betrayed when it was done betraying. We can act the same way as Assyria and put ourselves in the same selfish position. This can involve behaviors that demand our rights but ignoring the rights of others and breaking promises. It is important that you remember that broken promises hurt your relationships with others and make you untrustworthy. You need to make it a priority to treat others with the same fairness that you expect for yourself.

There was a small number of faithful people in Israel that continued to look to God for mercy and strength. These people asked for mercy and strength while asking God to be their salvation in times of trouble. This was their call to God for deliverance from their oppression. These people remembered that their enemies ran at the sound of God's voice and fled when God appeared. They knew that God was able to strip the army of Assyria. We need this same faith today.

Isaiah does provide a lovely picture of what is going to come for those that are faithful to God in Isaiah 33:5-6. The Lord will make Zion his home of justice and righteous one day even though he currently lives in heaven. When God does make his home in Zion, he will be our foundation. We will be able to get salvation, wisdom, and knowledge from God, but you must remember that fear of the Lord is our treasure.

While the vision of the future is bright, the current situation for Israel during Isaiah's time was dim. Warriors wept in public and ambassadors cried in disappointment. The land of Israel was mourning while Lebanon was in shame. Instead of fruitful, productive areas, the land was becoming deserts. Yet God did promise to punish Assyrian for their actions. He promised "Now, I will stand up. Now I will show my power and might." in Isaiah 33:10. Then Assyria will not be able to produce fruits and crops and will turn on itself.

The sinners in Jerusalem lived in fear because the presence of the Lord appeared as an all-consuming fire that devours evil. The sinners in Jerusalem did not want to walk upright and speak what is right. They knew that God wanted them to live with better ways. Isaiah gave multiple examples in Isaiah 33:15 of how to demonstrate righteousness including honesty, fairness, and rejecting fraud and plotting. The last example can be one of the hardiest to do: refuse to shut your eyes to evil. God will supply the needs of those who live for him by living righteously and uprightly.

When we are able to see God in all his splendor, we will no longer remember why our small earthly troubles worried us so much. We will no longer see the people that caused us trouble as powerful. Zion will be a place of holy festivals that is quiet and secure. The Lord will be a source of protection that no enemy can surpass. God will be our judge, king, and lawgiver. It will be a time when God will care for us so that none of his children are forgotten.

A Message for the Nations

Isaiah had a message for all nations of the earth. God is enraged against the nations and all of the armies. He promised to completely destroy the armies. He painted a picture that we have seen throughout the years with war: unburied dead with the stench of rotting bodies and blood flowing.

Additionally, God promises that Edom is marked for destruction because of their opposition to God and his people. Edom will be filled with burning pitch, covered with fire, and will burn forever as revenge for all its actions against Israel. The land will be deserted and will be called the Land of Nothing. The land will be overrun with thorns, nettles, and thistles where only wildlife will roam. The land will be deeded to the animals who will possess it forever.

Hope for Restoration

Chapter 35 begins a vision of beauty and encouragement. A beautiful picture of God's final kingdom is presented in contrast to the messages of judgment. God will establish his justice and destroy all evil when he establishes his final kingdom. Isaiah paints a picture of peace that will begin after God judges all people for their actions.

The land will be glad and even wastelands will rejoice. Wastelands will be filled with flowers while deserts will become green. This news is meant to strengthen the tired and encourage the weak. We need to remember Isaiah's message for those with fearful hearts, "Be strong, and do not fear, for your God is coming to destroy your enemies. He is coming to save you." Isaiah 35:4. God is going to heal the blind, deaf, lame, and mute when he comes to make Zion his home.

A great road is going to go through the land that was formerly deserted but turned into a lush green place. The road will be named the Highway of Holiness because no evil-minded people are going to be able to travel on it. No dangers will be present on it and only the redeemed will be able to use it. It will be used to enter Jerusalem so that the redeemed can praise God. There will be no sorrow and mourning. The road will be a place of joy and gladness. It is a beautiful image of what to expect when God returns.

Chapter 6
HISTORY

ISAIAH 36 - ISAIAH 39

I saiah 36 begins with an account of the attack from Assyria. It occurred in the fourteenth year of King Hezekiah's reign, 701 B.C. The fortified towns of Judah were conquered by Assyria. King Sennacherib of Assyria then sent his chief of staff to confront King Hezekiah in Jerusalem with a huge Assyrian army. The Assyrians went to the aqueduct near the road and waited for Jerusalem to send officials. King Hezekiah sent Eliakim, the palace administrator, Shebna, court secretary, and Joah, the royal historian, to speak with Assyrian's chief of staff.

The Assyrian field commander gave a message to the three men for King Hezekiah. It was a taunt for King Hezekiah. Assyria mocked Hezekiah's reliance on Egypt to keep their promise in addition to his trust in God. Hezekiah had great trust in Pharaoh's promise to aid Israel against Assyria. Pharaoh was not worthy of the trust and did not keep his promise. There are times that we put our trust in institutions or people instead of God like King Hezekiah was doing concerning Assyria.

Assyria did not know or understand Judah's religion and mistaken King Hezekiah's actions to eliminate idol worship as an insult to God.

Assyrians used their words to twist King Hezekiah's actions and put them in a bad light. Some of the people then questioned whether God would protect them if their King had insulted God. This is a common tool of Satan and he will use anyone he can. He attempts to confuse or deceive you. Confusion causes you to be ineffective tools for spreading God's word. Assyrians' words caused doubt and confusion which allowed the people to falter further in faith and distrust God.

Then the Assyrians made their demands: Judah had to make a bargain with the King Assyria. The commander intimidated the three representatives for Judah by comparing the size and strength of Judah's army to the size and strength of the Assyrian Army. The commander ended his speech by demoralizing Judah. It was an attempt to convince the People of Judah that God turned against them and the people's best option was surrendering. He was saying that God was telling Assyria to attack and destroy Judah. Isaiah was actively countering this claim at the time by spreading the promise that God would not allow Assyria to destroy Jerusalem. Satan continues to use this same tactic with us. Satan will use people or other medias to try convincing you that God has turned against you. Despite Satan's tactics, God is your salvation and not your enemy.

Judah's representatives' response was a reminder that the conversation should be in Aramaic, the international language of the Near East at that time. It was customary used in diplomacy and commerce. The representatives spoke and understood Aramaic while the common people would not. The Assyrian representative was purposely speaking in Hebrew so that the people around them could understand him and spread his message of doom to the masses. Assyrian's representative then addressed the people on the wall in Hebrew and purposely scares them with the threat of attack. He ends with a mock of their trust in God. He was continuing his plan to demoralize the people so that the people would encourage Hezekiah to make peace with Assyria. Satan will use the same tactic with you when you are facing him. He will try to demoralize you and make you question your loyalty in God.

God does protect those who genuinely believe in him and rely on him. The Northern Kingdom fell to Assyria because it stopped looking to God, but Judah did contain a remnant that looked to God which is why Jerusalem was rescued. Sadly, the three men that represented King Hezekiah were not very sure of God's protection of Judah. They tore their clothes and put on burlap in despair before they returned to King Hezekiah to inform him of the Assyrians' words.

Even King Hezekiah felt despair at the report of the Assyrians' words and did the same thing as his representatives. King Hezekiah then went to the Temple of the Lord while wearing burlap after he sent the three representatives to Isaiah (Isaiah 37:1-2). The three men brought the following message to Isaiah from King Hezekiah:

> Today is a day of trouble, insults, and disgrace. It is like when a child is ready to be born, but the mother has no strength to deliver the baby. But perhaps the Lord your God has heard the Assyrian Chief of Staff, sent by the king to defy the living God, and will punish him for his words. Oh, pray for those of us who are left! Isaiah 37:3-4

While Hezekiah saw the situation as hopeless, he did go to Isaiah for help and pray to God. Hezekiah was full of despair but did not lose hope in God. Hezekiah was turning to God by going to the Temple himself and sending his people to seek aid from Isaiah. God does help those who turn to Him in times of trouble.

Isaiah's response to Hezekiah's request was to not be disturbed by the words of Assyria. God was going to ensure that the Assyrian messenger would not be a threat and would be called back to Assyria where he would die. God's plan was already in motion. God had

Ethiopia ready to be the reason to save Judah. Hezekiah did not know what God had planned and acted properly by praying to God.

Sennacherib made sure to continue his threats and mocks with a message to King Hezekiah before he returned to fight Ethiopia's army. Hezekiah went to the Lord's Temple after reading the message. Hezekiah then prayed to God and recognized God's holiness, power, and sovereignty. He expresses that there are no other gods and the nations that had fallen to Assyria were not worshiping gods. Hezekiah ends his prayer with a request for God to rescue Judah from Assyria so that all kingdoms of the earth would know that God was the only God.

Due to King Hezekiah's prayer, God had Isaiah send a message to the king regarding King Sennacherib. It was a message against King Sennacherib. It was a message of the Lord's power and plan to counteract the Assyrian king's claim of power. King Sennacherib defied God with his boast. Isaiah reassures in Isaiah 37:26 that God planned it all and is making it all happen. God knows all about us including where we stay, when we will come and go, and even when we rage against him (Isaiah 37:28). Isaiah promises that the Lord will control the Assyrian king and will force him to return on the road that he came. The sign of proof from God for this message was a promise that the people would not have to plant new crops for two years. God was going to plant the crop so that the people would be able to harvest from crops that had grown up and sprung up by itself. There is the additional promise that the remaining people left in Judah would put down roots and flourish.

God promised that the Assyrian army would not enter Jerusalem. There was going to be no battle or march of the other army around Jerusalem. God promises to defend and protect Jerusalem. The angel of the Lord killed 185,000 Assyrian soldiers that night. King Sennacherib broke camp and returned to Nineveh after waking up and finding corpses everywhere. God kept his promises and protected Jerusalem without the remaining people of Judah having to do anything because King Hezekiah went to God in prayer when trouble came. We need to be like King Hezekiah and go to God in prayer with our troubles instead of trying to deal with them ourselves or with earthly assistance.

Chapter 37 ends with the fulfillment of Isaiah prophecy that King Sennacherib would die. Two of Sennacherib's sons killed him with their swords in the temple of Nisroch while Sennacherib was in Nineveh. Esarhaddon becomes the next king of Assyria after the two sons that killed Sennacherib escape to the land of Ararat.

Chapter 38 begins with the news of Hezekiah becoming deathly ill. Isaiah does go to visit him and gives him a message. It is not a good message. Isaiah tells King Hezekiah that the Lord says "Set your affairs in order, for you are going to die. You will not recover from this illness." (Isaiah 38:1). Hezekiah turns to God again and asks that God remembers his faithfulness. God then instructs Isaiah to return to Hezekiah to tell him that due to his prayer and tears, he will get fifteen more years of life. God promises to continue to defend the city of Jerusalem. God's sign of proof was causing the sun's shadow to move ten steps backward on the sundial. Hezekiah continues to be a good example for us to follow. Even though God planned for Hezekiah to die from the illness, God changed his plan when Hezekiah went to him in prayer. Our first move should be the one that Hezekiah did when he received news of impending death, go to God.

Hezekiah writes a poem of praise when he is well again to praise God for extending his life. Hezekiah knew that his prayer was the reason for God's deliverance and forgiveness. He looked to heaven for help and admitted that he was in trouble to God. Hezekiah sees that God's discipline is good because it "leads to life and health" (Isaiah 38:16). Hezekiah sees that God's decision showed him how precious and wonderful life was. He learned from the experience and looked forward to praising God while alive and telling the younger generation of God's faithfulness during his additional time on earth. Look for the lesson from difficult times and see if there is a reason for the experience instead of just complaining about it.

The king of Babylon sent his best wishes and a gift to Hezekiah soon after Hezekiah recovered. Hezekiah was foolish and showed the Babylonian envoys everything in his treasure-houses, armory, and royal treasures. Due to Hezekiah's foolishness, God instructed Isaiah to tell Hezekiah that everything in the palace would be carried off to Babylon. Some of Hezekiah's sons would be taken to Babylon in exile where they would be eunuchs in the Babylon's palace. Hezekiah did not pray to God to change his plans but accepted Isaiah's message from God as good because Hezekiah was happy that there would be peace and security during his lifetime. He only went to God in prayer when he was in trouble but did not go to God when others were in trouble. Hezekiah should have prayed for those that would be captured by Babylon instead of just caring about his own peace and security.

This is where Isaiah historical telling of the times stops. Isaiah 36 through 39 tells of many historical events that occurred while Isaiah was prophet for Judah. At the end of Isaiah 39, only a remnant of the people remain in Judah and there is promise of another exile.

Chapter 7

MESSAGES OF HOPE

ISAIAH 40-48

T he last twenty-five chapters of Isaiah were written during the end of Isaiah's ministry and focus on the future events for Judah. This includes the news of Jesus Christ and the coming of the new heaven and earth. We have had Jesus Christ show himself as our messiah, but we are still waiting on Isaiah's foretelling of when God will completely restore his people in the new heaven and earth. This section of Isaiah is a message of Hope in a multitude of ways.

Isaiah starts with a promise that God would release Israel from captivity in Chapter 40. This message served as a message of comfort and encouragement to God's people when they were in captivity and exile. It promises that the Lord would vindicate them and judge his enemies, but it took a long time. You can use this chapter in a similar way and use it to comfort and encourage yourself when you are in times of trouble. The first two verses focus on the fact that God does want to reassure you that he is there to provide comfort and encouragement. You can look to God's word, his presence, and fellowship for comfort and encouragement when you are having hard times. You will not always be saved from your adversities. Judah had almost two hundred years of trouble including seventy years of exile before God returned them to

Judah. The greatest comfort is that when you leave this earth, you will be with God.

Isaiah instructs Judah to prepare a way for the Lord in Isaiah 40:3-5. We should do as Isaiah instructed them and prepare the way for the Lord today. It is told in imagery that can be hard to understand because we do not consider land the same way that Isaiah did. The wilderness, wastelands, valleys, mountains, hills, curves, and rough places were a hindrance to an easy path. They are obstacles that prevent the spread of God's word. Our life trials and sufferings can be a hindrance when we allow them to stop us from preparing the way for God. Life trials and sufferings should be used for personal growth and deepening our relationship in God.

The few verses that follow are meant to show the difference between us and God. We are compared to grass and flowers to demonstrate our fragility and limited time. The word of God is the opposite and stands forever. Remember to go to God's word for comfort and aid before human resources. The words of human experts and opinions can in no way compare to what you can find in God's word. Isaiah promises that God will come in power and rule us one day. He will reward his people and care for us.

Most of Chapter 40 is used by Isaiah to show that God has no equal. God is the only being that can create, sustain, and help his people. No one advises, teaches, or leads God. He created our earth and sees all of us on it. He is all-powerful and controls all things. We like to think that we understand God and his power but there is nothing that we truly have that we can compare to him. Unlike the other religions, we and Jews do not attempt to create an image of God because we accept that we do not know what he looks like. The chapter ends with Isaiah lecturing us on our attitude in thinking that we can question God. We are like Judah and question whether God actually sees our troubles. It is a little ridiculous when you consider that God is all-powerful and all-knowing. When things do not go the way that we want, we question His knowledge and role. He does not ignore you but is doing as he knows it should be. Isaiah 40:28 does say "Have you never heard? Have you never understood? The Lord is the everlasting God, the Creator of all the Earth. He never grows weak or weary. No one can measure the depths of his understanding." God has unending power and strength and does provide power and strength to his people when they are in need. You can always go to God for power and strength when you are feeling weak. When you keep in mind that God never weakens, it makes it easier to trust in him for your strength. Sometimes it seems easier to lean on our own understanding and forget that God is greater. When you trust in God, he will strengthen you so that you can endure life's difficulties. You might not have your difficulties solved in the way that you desire, but he does provide the strength so that you can face them in the way that he planned. He provides strength not complete understanding nor wish fulfillment.

Help for Israel

The Lord is the alpha and omega and uses everything on Earth, including a pagan ruler, to protect and care for his people. God called a future king of Persia into his service and would help put him in a position to help Israel get out of captivity. Isaiah reassures Israel that they were God's chosen ones and God promised not to throw them away. We sometimes need Isaiah's message to Israel in Isaiah 41:10. God is with us so we should not be afraid. You should not be discouraged because the Lord is our God. God promises to strengthen, help, and hold you up. You are representing God to the modern world like Israel represented God to the world during Isaiah's time. Israel went into captivity because they failed to do their duty of showing God to their world. Take steps to ensure that you represent God to our world. Even in times of trouble, God is with you and will protect you.

God is all powerful and can defeat your enemies for you when you go to him with your troubles. He can confuse and humiliate your enemies or prevent them from succeeding in their plans. The Lord is right by your side when you are under attack. He is ready to fight for you if you allow Him. He is your Redeemer and will keep you safe. You do not need to fear hard times because you are never alone.

The Lord will provide the needs of the poor and needy. God promised to never abandon Israel and will not abandon you either. God would perform miraculous actions such planting trees in a barren desert to ensure that the people knew it was from him. God still performs these actions but uses modern things to ensure that his people are cared for.

Chapter 41 ends with a good case against idols. You need to remember that the worship of idols has not gone away, and you can be as guilty of worshiping idols as the people of Judah. Our idols are not statutes but are money, career, or anything that can be prioritized before God. God does not beat around the bush and straight up tells his people to present their case for their idols in Isaiah 41:21. The idols of the nations surrounding Israel in Isaiah's time were unable to do what God did for Israel, but they still were tempting to the people of Israel. Idols of the modern world are still tempting and like the Isrealite's idols are not able to provide what God can provide to you. God promised to provide help to Israel, and He promises to help you. Idols are just foolish, worthless things that prevent you from putting our trust completely in God.

A Chosen Servant form God

The first nine verses of Chapter 42 describe the messenger that the Lord promised Israel which later is revealed to be Jesus in the New Testament. The messenger is described as gentle, encouraging, just, and honest. He is God's chosen one and is strengthened by God. This messenger would lead to instruction being spread throughout the lands and justice prevailing. The messenger would demonstrate the Lord's righteousness. He would be given to Israel as a symbol of God's covenant with Israel. The messenger would be a light to guide the nations, open the eyes of the blind, and free captives from prison. God's promise was accomplished with Jesus. You should take Isaiah 42: 6-7 as a call for yourself and work on ensuring that your life demonstrates God's righteousness and acts as a light for God's message.

Song of Praise

The middle part of chapter 42 is a song of praise for the Lord for what he will do for Israel. One line really resonates: Sing his praises from the ends of the Earth! Your goal should be that everyone on Earth knows and worships God. The Lord is a mighty warrior that will crush his enemies. God will protect and lead those who follow him but those who forsake him for idols will not be safe.

Failure to Listen and See

Chapter 42 ends with a lecture to Israel for not listening or seeing. Israel is called deaf and blind. Isaiah 42:20 describes Israel as seeing and recognizing what is right but refusing to act on it and hearing with their ears but not really listening. A description that can often fit everyone. There are a lot of people who know what is right but do not do want is right. It is easy to find people who hear but do not listen. Sadly, we who believe in God are just as bad as atheists in these bad habits. God allowed his people to be robbed, enslaved, and imprisoned because they did not listen or see so that they could learn their lesson. Learn from their mistakes, you can avoid hard lessons for the same actions. God will allow times of trouble to come if you repeat Israel's mistake and fail to walk in his path. Israel had to go through some rough times because they refused to understand or learn their lesson. You have them as an example and do not have to do the same thing.

God's Mercy

Even though everyone fails to perfectly obey God's laws and put idols before him, God shows mercy and love. He would free Israel from captivity and restore them after they went through times of trouble. God provides mercy to them due to His love. Chapter 43 gives the message of God's mercy and love for everyone.

It starts with a call for Israel to listen to the Lord and not to be afraid. You should treat this like a call to yourself. We are like Israel who lost our way and do not follow God completely with our hearts. Listen to the Lord and do not fear him. God is always with us and fear is unnecessary. He is with us when we are going through rivers of difficulty and fires of oppression. He will not stop us from having times of troubles, but God does protect you so that you do not drown nor be consumed by the flames. You can grow stronger when you go through hard times and rely on God to protect you.

God considers Israel and us as precious, honored, and loved. He will protect us and ensure the safety of his children. Those who do not believe in God do not have his protection, like Egypt was not protected from Persia. God protects his children even though we do foolish things and move away from him, but we need to give our love and loyalty to him.

Israel was chosen to be the Lord's servant and tasked with the job of telling the world about God. When Jesus died and created the way for gentiles, we accepted the title and task that God assigned to his people. You are the Lord's servant and have the responsibility of telling the world about God. You are to be good examples of his word so that those who do not believe can see God's love with your words and actions. You are chosen to know God, believe in him, and rely on him. He is the only God in our world. In a world of options, it is important to always remember that he is the one and only God and your role is to spread the message of his love.

In Isaiah's time, the Lord had done many miracles for Israel in the past including parting the water and allowing Israel to escape Egypt after captivity. The Lord promises to do an even bigger miracle. God would deliver Israel from captivity when they cried out for deliverance like their ancestors did in Egypt. When Isaiah is telling them this news of promised deliverance, Israel was not going to God for forgiveness. They were sinning but not seeking forgiveness. We can be the same way and refuse to seek forgiveness at times. It is important to remember that Israel had been warned that their actions were leading them to trouble, but they refused to listen. It is better to learn from their mistakes instead of making the same mistakes.

Israel was forgetting that only God can remove our sins. We can fall into the same trap and not take our sins to God so that they can be removed. Once you take your sins to God, he completely forgets them and does not hold them against you anymore. Everyone sins and is on the pathway of destruction, but God has chosen to provide mercy to his children. God's children will consist of people who proudly proclaim to belong to him, descendants of Jacob, those who write the Lord's name on their hands, and those who take that name of Israel. God will bless his children and save them from the path of destruction.

Idols

Isaiah gives a message from the Lord in Isaiah 44 concerning the foolishness of idols. This chapter contains one of those well-known lines Isaiah 44:6 - I am the first and the Last; there is no other God. This is a line that most Christians and even some atheists can say from memory. It is the first line in God's message against idols. This line is a nice summary in that it defines that God is the only God and idols are not gods.

God is the being that created our world and us. He has protected his people since ancient times and continues to protect us. God is our rock. Yet foolish people make idols from worthless objects. These idols are worshiped but do nothing for their followers. Idols are made by people while God created us. When Israel or you turn to idols instead of God, you are relying on something that cannot deliver the protection and help that God does provide. It is a pathway of disgrace and shame. When you turn to idols, you are letting pride in your own creations take the place of your love for God.

Humans turn God's creations, such as wood or stone, into idols from their own work instead of recognizing that God created all of it. We show our ignorance when we use the things that God provides for our needs to create idols. Israel made idols from the wood and stone that God gave them for food and shelter, and we turn money, fame, and power into idols instead of using them as God intended. When you do not prioritize God, you are more likely to worship idols. When you do not try to see God or turn your thoughts to God, you are more likely to worship the things that God gives you. It is foolish to trust something that cannot protect you over God who created you.

If you remember to keep your eyes and mind on God, worshiping idols will seem foolish and is easier to avoid.

God's Promises

Even though Israel turned away from God, God did not forget them. God would have his people returned to him. God sweeps away our sins and scatters our offenses so that we can be with him. You should worship him for his mercy and glorify his name for his blessings. God made all things and shows that all others are unable to foretell the future. Isaiah assured Israel that Jerusalem and Judah would be restored and rebuilt. God ensured that Cyrus would command the rebuilding of Jerusalem and the restoration of the Temple before they were destroyed. He showed that he is all-knowing in Isaiah 44.

In Isaiah 45, Isaiah tells about Cyrus who ruled 150 years after Isaiah's prophecies. Cyrus is a gentile ruler but is also the Lord's anointed one. God would empower Cyrus so that he would be able to rebuild Jerusalem and free the Jews so that they could return to Jerusalem. God did not give victory to Cyrus because of what Cyrus did but gave him power so that God's children could be saved and restored. God sends good times and bad times. Cyrus needed to be powerful and wealthy so that God's people could have good times after years of bad times.

You should not question why God does what he does because he is the one who made all living things. It is foolish to question our creator for his purpose. Cyrus, a gentile, was created and raised to fulfill God's righteous purpose. God guided Cyrus actions like he guides everyone. God continues to use those who do not believe in him to fulfill righteous purposes. It is important to remember God's promises to protect us, but we should not question his steps in leading our lives since he is our all-knowing creator. You need to remember that you can only see the small picture while God sees the big picture.

Conversion of Gentiles

God promised that Israel would rule the Egyptians, the Ethiopians, and the Sabeans. This is because God is with them and he is the only God. Isaiah tells us that our God works in mysterious ways. He ensures that those who create idols are humiliated and disgraced while he saves us with eternal salvation. When you choose salvation with God, you are protected from humiliation and disgrace. Isaiah's words of eternal salvation are important because Israel focused on temporal salvation from God at this time. It is easy to be like Israel and look to God for help in your immediate wants and needs instead of remembering the eternal salvation that God is providing.

God made everything including heaven and earth. He made earth so that we could live on it and have what we need. It is repeated often in Isaiah that God tells Isaiah "I am the Lord, and there is no other." God is proud and makes bold promises that we need to remember. He tells his children to seek him because he does not hide from us. God speaks truth and righteousness on which you should rely on.

God calls all fugitives from surrounding nations to come to him and turn from the idols of the world. He wants all to come to him, a righteous God and Savior. The whole world should look to God for salvation because there is no other god. Up to this point, salvation from God seemed to be only for Israel but Isaiah is firm in his words that God wants to provide salvation for everyone. If you were raised in Sunday school you might recognize a line from Isaiah 45:23; every knee will bend to me, and every tongue will praise me. It is widely recognized that the new testament's intended audience is gentiles, but Isaiah has a message meant for all, not just Israel.

Babylon

Isaiah uses two of Babylon's gods to show inadequacy of the false gods of other nations. False gods are unable to move or save themselves unlike our God. Our God protects his people from conception to death. God made us and cares for us while the false gods are created by people. Only God knows the future and can provide the comfort, peace, and security that we seek. God has a plan and is ensuring that what needs to be accomplished is in the works.

Israel was not doing what was right in the eyes of the Lord when

Isaiah was alive. They were being stubborn just like we often are and as Isaiah 46:13 describes are so far from doing right. God assures us that he is ready to set things right immediately and he is waiting on us to do what is right. When you decide to move towards him, he is ready to show his glory just like he was ready to save Jerusalem then.

Then Isaiah moved to another big prediction that would not occur for more than 150 years. Isaiah predicts that the days that Babylon would rule would be numbered. When Babylon's days as a mighty force ended, it would never gain power again. God would use Babylon to punish Judah for their sins and then have them be defeated. Babylon showed no mercy but did show a pride that led to their defeat and loss of power.

The people of Babylon are like a lot of people in our own society. They were caught up in the pursuit of power and pleasure. They felt secure and proud in their position in the world. So many people of our time feel the same things. God brought such calamity to Babylon that we only hear about it in relation to history. Babylon was blatantly doing public wickedness because of their false sense of security. Some people are in the same place and need to learn the lesson that Babylon learned the hard way. Babylon was unable to charm their way out of punishment from God. God is wanting your obedience not your charm nor money.

Another source of help that people go to instead of God is experts of this world. Babylon's experts were astrologers and stargazers who claimed to be able to do magic. Babylon relied on these individuals to protect them from danger. You can rely on others in a similar fashion instead of going to God with your problems. The astrologers and stargazers were not able to save themselves from God's wrath, much less protect the other people. It is the same with the individuals that you go to for help instead of going to God.

Stubbornness of Humans

The people of Judah were not keeping their promise to God. They had a false sense of security based on the assumption that God would protect them even though they were sinning against God. The people of Judah were relying on their heritage city's reputation instead of relying on God. Christian can fall into the same situation and rely on their status as a Christian instead of relying on God. A personal relationship with God is the key for true security from God.

The people of Judah continued to call Jerusalem the holy city, but they were not doing what was needed to ensure that the city would be protected. The people were stubborn and obstinate. They were described as unbending as iron and as hard as bronze. God foretold of many events and all of them have come true, but the people of Judah continued to look to idols instead of God. Stubbornness is a trait that has become so common and acceptable that we tend to not see how it is wrong to be stubborn with God. You can take a lesson that the people of Judah did not take and replace stubbornness with trust in God.

God promises new predictions that he would fulfill to show that He controls everything. Humans are sinners at birth and by nature fight against obedience. God refines us through times of suffering and trouble to teach us how to be better. God is the only God and does not share glory with idols. We are created for his works and to ensure that his glory is seen.

God is the only God who is the Alpha and Omega. He created our world and the heaven which we will go to when we die. He uses believers and non-believers to ensure that his predictions are fulfilled. Isaiah predicted that God would use a pagan king named Cyrus two hundred years before it would occur. God used Cyrus to stop Babylon even though Cyrus was a non-believer. God can strengthen non-believers when their actions help fulfill God's purpose. It is often assumed that God is only there for those who follow him, but everyone is here for God's purpose.

God told Isaiah to tell the People of Judah that God was there to teach us what is good for us and lead us along paths that we should follow. We are meant to listen to his commands. When you do so, you are able to have an easier way, but you make your path harder when you show stubbornness towards his directions. You are looking for punishment and hard times when you do not listen to God's commands and fight his path for you. God does not want to destroy humans, but we fight against his teachings and instructions like rebellious teenagers.

God assures the people of Judah that they would be freed from captivity in Babylon before Babylon was a military power. God would redeem his servants and provide for them as they returned home. God provides the impossible such as water in the desert. He continues to provide the impossible to us. God does not provide peace for the wicked. It is important that you have a relationship with God to get comfort, security, and relief from him. People who look to God for peace in times of trouble but do not trust are futilely asking. God provides to those who have turned towards him and away from the world.

Isaiah predicted many wonderful events for the people of Judah despite their stubbornness. They would be saved and God would continue to provide for them. God continues to provide for those who are his children and learn from him. God uses all of us to fulfill his purpose and he has a plan for us. You need to look to him for your path.

Chapter 8

JESUS: OUR REDEEMER

ISAIAH 49-59

G od had to provide a redeemer so that we could be eternally saved. The sacrificial system did not provide a way to clean all sin away. God tells us of the future redeemer that he would send so that salvation could be accomplished in these chapters.

Messiah

God created the Messiah, who is also called the Lord's Servant, for all nations. Isaiah is clear that God called the Messiah before his birth. The Messiah is meant to be God's weapon. He had words of judgment that are as sharp as a sword and is a sharp arrow in God's quiver. God hid the Messiah from humans for many years and waited until he decided it was time to give him to us. The Messiah was created to bring Israel back to God and be a light to the gentiles. He brings salvation to all the earth and not just Israel.

At times, it seems like we prioritize the idea that Jesus was a gift to us, but remember that Jesus was always the part of God that would provide the salvation. Yes, we need salvation to be able to be with God due to our sinful nature. Ultimately Jesus is the light that the world needed to spread the glory of God to all the nations.

God's Power and Mercy

The Lord told Isaiah that he would respond to Israel at just the right time. God promised to help Israel on the day of salvation and he would protect them and give his people the land that he had promised to their ancestors. God would establish the land of Israel and give it to his people again. The northern part of their land had already been lost and the southern part would be lost in the following years. There has been a fight over the land that God promised to Abraham for centuries. In 1948, Israel proclaimed itself as a state using the land that is referenced in the bible. This occurred after Jews were advised to return to the area for about two decades. It was not a quick process, but God has given the land back to Abraham's children. It is as Isaiah 49:12 says "See, my people will return from far away, from lands to the north and west, and from as far south as Egypt."

God comforts his people and has compassion for their sufferings. He does it for the Jews in their battle for their lost land and he does it for all of us in our times of trouble. Jerusalem has seen that while it was deserted for a time, it was not forgotten by God. God brought his children back to Jerusalem after their years of captivity in Babylon and brought them back again in our more modern times. God is like a loving mother who never forgets her child even when the child is being punished or is enduring consequences of his or her bad choices. God will never forget us and will provide comfort and compassion just like he did for his people of Jerusalem.

God promised the people that were worshiping idols and refusing to obey his commandments that they would have to live with the consequences of their actions. Their descendants would return to

Israel and be protected from their enemies. The children born in exile would return and the land would be overcrowded. This occurred with the people born in Babylon after the King of Babylon allowed them to return and it occurred after World War I when Jews were spread through all nations.

God would ensure that other nations would do the necessary steps to return his children to their land. Nations would free slaves and return plunder so that the city of Jerusalem could be restored. Kings and queens would serve the people and take care of the people's needs instead of forcing them to fight for their needs. This is all done because God uses believers and non-believers to show that he is all-powerful and the one true God.

Israel would be taken into captivity because of their sins not because God chose not to fight for them. It was a consequence of their choice to forget God and put their reliance on other nations instead of God. God was there but Israel rejected God and Israel had to deal with the consequence. Israel would not answer his call or obey his word. We can often be like Israel. We blame God for our situation in times of trouble instead of recognizing that our choice to rely on money or our pride led to a poor situation. We often reject God just like Israel but expect to be rescued from the consequence. God promised to restore Israel and He kept His promise. God will keep his promise to restore us too, but it is better to learn from their mistakes and rely on God not worldly things.

Isaiah, unlike Israel, relied on God to protect him and show him the right path. He listened to God instead of turning away from him. Isaiah faced mockery and bullying from others without reacting in anger due to his faith in God's power to protect him. He knew that God would not allow him to be disgraced and would destroy his enemies. We need to be like Isaiah, determined to do God's will despite the obstacles of our world. Isaiah was an obedient servant to God and declares in Isaiah 50:9 that the Lord was on his side. Israel was not listening to Isaiah's words from God. They were determined to be self-sufficient which leads to them walking in darkness. We can act the same way and try to rely on our own abilities instead of God. Isaiah 50:11 tells us what happens to those that do not trust and rely on God, they will have torment. Only God can fully protect you from the troubles that our world has in it.

Isaiah addresses the faithful remnant in Isaiah 51. These were the people in Israel who were trusting and relying on God. Isaiah comforts them with the reminder that Abraham was only one person, but God created a great nation from him due to his trust and reliance on God. With the number of Christians seeming to diminish, take the same comfort that a few can do so much when they remain faithful to God. God promised that he would not leave Israel in captivity forever and would comfort her and provide mercy after they saw the consequence of their sin. God does provide mercy and justice to his children even when they reject him. We often have to live with the consequence of our sins but God is there to be our salvation. Our world will not last forever but God's salvation is forever. What you know will eventually die. God is your only hope.

Isaiah's word of advice to those who follow God's laws is to not be afraid of what people will say to us. God's righteousness is forever and those who scorn and insult are temporary. Our eternal salvation is more important than the words of the people around us. You need to focus on trusting and relying on God. God is able to perform miraculous actions and can protect those who are faithful to him. Isaiah assured them that Israel would be returned to Israel filled with joy and gladness. The bible is filled with so many miracles from God that it seems foolish to not trust God to care for you.

Israel did not fear God but was afraid of Babylon. This was the reason that they turned to other nations for help. We have the same tendency to fear people more than we fear God. God has more power than the people that we often fear. God has the ability to defeat our enemies. God created the earth and humans, yet we tend to fear God's creations more than God himself. It is important to remember both

God's mercy and God's power. When you remember them, you can see how your fear of people is an overaction when you trust God.

Instead of Jerusalem being a good example of what God's holy city should do, Jerusalem was filled with fear of a human enemy. The city that would have been prosperous, if it had trusted God to protect it, faced desolation and destruction because it did not trust God. The city was left in ruin and most of the people of Judah were taken into captivity. Even though Jerusalem did not rely on God, God was not going to forget about his holy city. He promised before it was even destroyed that He would restore Jerusalem and destroy its enemy. He will do the same for us. When you sin and are in the consequence of your sin, God will be there and has a way to restore you when you turn to him.

Jerusalem's Deliverance

God calls Jerusalem, called Zion in chapter 52, to wake up, clothe itself with strength and take its place of honor. It will be a place of honor where sinners will not be able to enter. God would restore the city of Jerusalem and redeem his people from slavery. God would call his people enslaved by Assyria and ensure that his people recognized his power to save them.

God would send messengers of good news of peace and salvation. The faithful remnant in Jerusalem would be joyful when the good news of God's redeeming of his people came to the city. He would show all the nations his power when he redeemed his people. The people enslaved would need to purify themselves and would leave their enslavement with no fear or anxiety. God protected his people and set a way for them to safely return to Jerusalem. The Jewish exiles would return to Jerusalem with guaranteed protection from a gentile king. God protected them by going ahead and by being behind them. He does the same thing with us. He has plans for you and will protect you by preparing your path, then he protects you by trailing behind you as you move on the path.

Messiah, the Lord's Suffering Servant

Lord assured the Jews and assures us that his servant will prosper and will be highly exalted. The Messiah will be disfigured and would startle the nations. He would make kings speechless and his story would spread. The Messiah is God's powerful arm but would come to us in a humble form. He was not going to be beautiful or majestic but would look like an average person. The Messiah is despised and rejected by his people. Even though we turn our back on him, the Messiah carries our weaknesses and sorrows. He was pierced for our rebellion, not as a punishment for his own sins. Isaiah foretells of the Messiah being beaten and whipped for our sins so that we can become healed. Isaiah compares us to lost sheep of God's while the Messiah is the servant that the Lord lays all of our sins on. It is foretold that the Messiah would be oppressed and treated harshly but would remain silent. Isaiah compares him to a lamb led to the slaughter in that he would be silent and not open his mouth. Messiah would be unjustly condemned and would die without children. He would not die in his old age but would be unjustly put to death in his mid-years. The Messiah would be sinless and honest, yet humans would bury him like a criminal in a rich man's grave. We know how these prophecies go because we read of their fulfillment in the New Testament with Jesus' death. Isaiah foretells these events hundreds of years before Jesus was born.

The Messiah's life was an offering for everyone's sin. The Lord's plan to save his children required that the Messiah go through grief and anguish. God told Isaiah that many would be counted as righteous due to the Messiah's experience. The Messiah bears all of our sins. Isaiah calls the Messiah a victorious soldier who exposes himself to death and bore the sins of many. We are the rebels that he interceded death for. Isaiah wrote this prophecy hundreds of years before the events of Jesus' death but they happened just as God told Isaiah so that we could be saved from our sin. God sent the Messiah to suffer so that we do not have to suffer what we deserve due to our sins. We can be restored and saved due to Christ's, the Messiah, fulfillment of chapter 52 and 53 of Isaiah.

Jerusalem and its Future Glory

Isaiah 54 begins with Isaiah comparing Jerusalem to a childless woman. This is a metaphor to show the city's shame and unfruitfulness. It quickly adds instruction to rejoice because God had plans to give the city blessing. Isaiah does explain that God did abandon his city for a short time because his children were blatantly sinning and refused to turn to him. God promised to return and take her back because of his everlasting love for his city. God punished the city due to their sin but promises to never punish his child by abandoning them again. We can take just as much reassurance from this promise as his promise to never flood the earth again. God promises mercy for Jerusalem and us from his anger at our sin.

Isaiah reassures the city that God would rebuild the city including its foundation, towers, gates, and walls. God will do the same for you when you turn to him and rely on him instead of yourself. It is not only the external aspects that God would repair but also internal aspects. God would ensure peace for the children, a just and fair government, and safety from enemies. God promises that they would live in peace and would be protected from attacks. God can provide you the same peace while you go through the trials of your lives. He will protect you from enemies just like Isaiah describes God will do for his city.

Lord's Salvation

Chapter fifty-five starts with a basic question: Is anyone thirty? It then immediately offers a drink to fulfill that thirst for free and offers a choice of wine or milk. Isaiah tells us that the free nourishment that we get from God is more important than the food that we purchase with money. Food meets our physical needs but only lasts a short time while the spiritual nourishment that we get from God fulfills our soul's needs and lasts forever. Instead of prioritizing your physical needs, you should prioritize your spiritual needs that start with salvation.

Isaiah provides three steps that you should take to get nourishment from God: come, listen, and seek God. You need to go to God with open ears so that you can hear his word because they give life. He loves you just as he loved King David and wants to provide all of your needs. He used David to show his power because David relied on God to provide for him through his trials which grew David's relationship with God. If you follow David's example and look to God during all times including trials, you will also show God's power with your lives.

It is easier for God to respond to you when you decide to remain near him. You are able to stay close to God when you continually seek him. Yes, God does forgive when his children wander away and sin. He is generous in both his mercy and his grace. It is a gift to be forgiven but it is also a gift to be able to spiritually grow by seeking God.

In verse eight and nine, Isaiah gives us God's words that explains why we are unable to comprehend God's plans.

> "My thoughts are nothing like your thoughts," says the Lord. "And my ways are far beyond anything you could imagine. For just as the heavens are higher than the earth, so my ways are higher than your ways and my thoughts higher than your thoughts." Isaiah 55:8-9 NLT

We often act like we can think like God and understand everything by questioning the purpose of bad events such as natural disasters and wars. We even will complain about trials as we go through them because we are unable to see the growth or benefits that come from trials until afterwards. It is very much a parent-child relationship that we continue to fight even as adults because our fight for control and independence causes us to forget that we are not equal with God. It is a hard choice to make, but you need to remember your place as the child and respect that God's plans and purpose is good for you even when it does not make sense to you at the moment.

God provides the water that our earth needs so that we can grow the food that we need. He provides not only our physical needs but also our spiritual needs with his word. He sends his word just like he sends water and both produce fruit. While water feeds the ground, God's word feeds us. When you allow the word of God to feed you, you are able to produce fruit by doing as the word says. When you live the word of God and live his purpose for you, you will have joy and peace in your lives. This does not mean that you will not have trials, but you can have joy and peace with your trials by relying on God and knowing that God will provide what is best for you.

God freely offers salvation and gives the option to come to him for it. Then you have the choice to listen and seek. You determine how fruitful you will be.

Blessings and Condemnation

Chapter fifty-six includes a message of blessings for all nations and condemnation for sinful leaders. We are instructed to be fair to all and do what is right and good. God promises that he will come to rescue us. God will bless those who do as he instructs, honor the sabbath days, and work to ensure that they do not sin. Isaiah tells us that God's blessing is for all people, not just the Jews. God says that he will bless foreigners who commit themselves to him and eunuchs who were not considered as equal. This means that God excludes no one from accepting the salvation that he offers. While God started as the God of the Jews, Isaiah gives the message in the Old Testament that God is for people of all races and social status.

While the New Testament is full of messages, mostly from Paul, that proclaim God's promises to bless and provide for all people, Isaiah is one of the few Old Testament books that provide a message of blessing for people other than Jews. God promised to provide a name and a place for the eunuchs even though society saw them as less than citizens. God also promised to bless any foreigner who did as the Jews were instructed and committed themselves to him. He promised them a place in his holy mountain before he sent Jesus. God proclaimed that his Temple is meant to be a house of prayer for all nations. It is verse Isaiah 56:8 that says it best with "For the Sovereign Lord, who brings back the outcasts of Israel, says: I will bring others, too, besides my people Israel." The New Testament can seem more applicable to Christians in comparison to the Old Testament. It is important that we remember that before Jesus, God already had his plan to provide for us and the Old Testament is just as important to us as the New Testament.

The last few verses of chapter fifty-six concern the watchmen which are the leaders of the nation of Israel. They are described as blind and ignorant who provide no warning to the people of the nation when dangers are approaching. Instead of doing their intended duty of protecting the people, the leaders are only intent on their own personal gain and doing what is best for them. The leaders do what they want such as drinking instead of being diligent and keeping watch for dangers. This is a good description of many of the leaders of the world today at all levels of authority. Instead of focusing on doing the duties originally designed for public servants and leaders of organizations, many leaders in our society are ignoring their responsibilities and focusing on personal wants and desires. God describes an apathy for people needs that we have become accustomed to tolerating within our current society.

Idol Worship

Isaiah returns to the topic of idol worship and how God condemns it in chapter fifty-seven. We are often like the people of Isaiah's time and worship our idols with great passion. They were sacrificing children in practices along with giving their idols offerings instead of worshiping God. When you turn to idols instead of God, you are being unfaithful and committing spiritual adultery. You are meant to be in an exclusive spiritual relationship with God, but you are breaking that commitment when you worship idols.

Isaiah lists ways that his people were worshiping idols but we do similar acts today. They were putting pagan symbols in their homes, making offers, and traveling to search for new idols. We put symbols such as images and statutes in our homes for ideals that have become our idols. We make offerings with our time and money to work, organizations, and other beliefs that can easily become idols for us. People travel all over the world seeking other religions or modern belief systems that fit what they want.

God promises to expose our good deeds to show that we cannot earn forgiveness for our sins. When you are confronted with the inability to rely on yourself, those idols' inability to provide the security and help that God provides when you rely on him becomes obvious. The frailty and powerlessness of idols comes to light in times of trouble. In times of trouble, you see God's strength and power.

God restores crushed spirits and revives courage to those who are humble and repentant. Yes, God does punish his children like all fathers do when children are disobedient but he promises that he will not always be angry. He promises to return to us so that he can heal, lead, and comfort us. He brings abundant peace to those he heals unlike those who continue to reject him. You have a choice. You can choose God and get comfort and peace from God or reject God and be restless and conflicted.

True Worship vs. False Worship

Isaiah had a message for the people of his time that is just as relevant to us today. The people were outwardly worshiping but their pious actions were not from a desire to have a relationship with God. It is one of the biggest problems that continue to afflict christians in our current society. The people were going to the Temple every day, participating in learning, acting righteous, and obeying the laws but they were doing it for the wrong reasons. A lot of people do the right actions and say the right words but do it for approvals from others not to get closer to God.

There are two aspects of true worship that Isaiah addresses: relationship with God and reaching out to others. It is more important that our purpose is to reach out to God when we pray and worship and not for pride or recognition. While personal aspects to grow your relationship with God is good, you also need to reach out to others. When you only consider your own relationship and not work on reaching out to others, you do not show God's love which is failure to do God's mission for you.

Isaiah lists a few ways that you can help others in Isaiah 58:6-7. You can free the wrongly imprisoned, help people that are oppressed or chained, share food with the hungry, help the homeless, donate clothing to the needy, and help relatives. God goes to those who do his work by helping those in need. So many Christian make comments that they do not feel God but they are not trying to reach out to those in need. You need to remember that you are the light in the darkness that surrounds our world. It is important that you spread that light.

As someone that grew up in the church, it is easy to get into the bad habit of doing worship in auto-pilot and not with a sincere heart. You go to church every week, go to bible study, listen to your christian music in the car, and read your bible but you do not have the proper motivation. You go through the motions but do not truly seek God. You can get so busy in life that instead of focusing on our relationship with God, you put in the bare minimal effort to "do" what you are told is important and forget about God's instructions to reach out to those in need. God promises to provide for you when you do his work. Life might not be easy when you focus on your relationship with God and helping those in need but it will be more fulfilling than when you worship on auto-pilot.

Chapter 58 finishes with the reminder to keep the Sabbath day holy. This can be a harder task due to the demands of some workplaces. When it is possible, you should be making Sunday a day of rest. While it is easy to logic that a short grocery shopping trip does not hurt anything, it takes away from the purpose of the day. There is a restoring power to going to church and a family dinner on Sunday. It allows you to rest and gathering with family is a way to bond and support each other. God is wise in giving us a day of rest to be healthier for the rest of the week.

Warnings Against Sin

Sin cuts us off from God. You have to turn from your sin and give it to God for God to listen to you. God cannot tolerate sin which is why you have to acknowledge and seek forgiveness before God can accept you. Chapter 59 lists the multitudes of ways that you can sin in this world. Sins range from murder to telling lies.

Isaiah 59:4-11 gives an astounding accurate description of our world even though they were written thousands of years ago. Here are some of the descriptions:

1. no one cares about being fair and honest
2. People's lawsuits are based on lies
3. conceive evil deeds
4. hatch deadly snakes
5. weave spiders' webs
6. nothing they do is productive
7. violence is their trademark
8. rush to commit murder
9. misery and destruction always follow them
10. don't know where to find peace
11. mapped out crooked roads
12. no justice among us
13. grope like the blind along a wall
14. growl like hungry bears
15. moan like mournful doves
16. look for justice, but it never comes
17. look for rescue, but it is far away

Sin does not make life easy or comfortable. It leads to misery, destruction, and uncertainty. The actions of sin are self-centered which causes trouble for society in general. God turns his back on those who live in sin because they are rebelling against him when they choose sin over him. When society is governed by sin, things are unfair, oppressive, dishonest, and lack justice. We need God to have a place within our government and society to remove the issues that come from sin.

God is the only one that can remove sin when his people seek repentance and forgiveness. God has the righteousness, salvation, vengeance, and divine passion that is necessary to defeat sin and its evil deeds. You need to respect God's name and glorify him. He is your only hope against sin and its deadly consequences. It is important that you remember God's promise to those who repent of sin that is given in

Isaiah 59:21 "My Spirit will not leave them, and neither will these words I have given you. They will be on your lips and lips of your children and children's children forever. I, the Lord, have spoken!" When you choose God, he becomes part of you.

Chapter 9

THE FUTURE KINGDOM

ISAIAH 60-66

Isaiah starts his prophecies of the future kingdom with a vision of Jerusalem in the last days. Jerusalem is directed to be a light for all the world to follow. God is shining his glory onto Jerusalem while the rest of the earth is covered in darkness. Isaiah foretells that all nations will come to Jerusalem due to its light and radiance. Merchants from all over the world will go to Jerusalem and bring their wealth to the city. People of other nations will worship God and bring him offerings. While we see so many people turning away from God in our current time, there will be a day that all nations will have people turning to God and Jerusalem. We just need to be patient and wait for God's timing.

In verses 8-9, Isaiah almost describes airplanes. Something flying like clouds to Israel similar to doves to their nests. The "ships" are going to Israel from the ends of the earth and from lands that trust in God. They will be bringing people of Israel home. Isaiah foretells of foreigners going to Israel to rebuild its towns. God's grace will provide mercy on Israel and have wealth come to Israel. Then God will destroy all nations that refuse to serve Israel. Israel's temple will be glorious and the enemies of Israel will serve it.

So many nations still despise and hate Jerusalem. They refuse to recognize it as the proper capital of Israel. Isaiah tells of Jerusalem being despised and hated with no one traveling through it. While Jerusalem has had a hard history and continues to have difficult relationships with many nations of the world, Isaiah promises that God will make it beautiful forever. The city will be a great joy to all generations. God will remove violence from its land and end the war that causes desolation and destruction that is present in its land. God will have salvation surrounding the city like city walls. It is a lovely image for a city and nation that is filled with so much violence and destruction. Only God can change circumstances to such extremes for those that put their faith in him.

Isaiah foretells that there will be a time when God will make it so that we do not need the sun nor the moon. God will provide us an everlasting light. When God provides an everlasting light to replace the sun and moon, he will also end our days of mourning. At the right time, God is going to make all his people righteous, plant them in a place of his planning. We will possess that land forever and God's small family will grow into a thousand people that will become a mighty nation. Lord knows the right time and you need to patiently wait for his promised future for those that put their faith in him.

Good News for Those who are Oppressed

Jesus quoted Isaiah 61:1-2 in the synagogue as written in Luke 4:18-19 to show that the Scripture has been fulfilled. Jesus was sent to bring good news to the poor and comfort the brokenhearted. He proclaimed that captives will be released and prisoners will be freed. A joyous blessing is promised in place of mourning and festive praise instead of despair.

Isaiah assures us that God loves justice and hates wrongdoing. God will faithfully reward his people when they endure suffering for injustice.

We have an everlasting covenant with God that he will provide for us even during our suffering. You might not be provided or rewarded in the ways that you expect but you need to remember that his thinking is higher than yours and he knows more than you do. God promises to bless his people.

The last two verses of chapter 61 are a bright promise of the future for those that are oppressed with sin. God will overwhelm them with joy from his or her relationship with him. He will dress them with salvation and drape his children with righteousness. God will show his justice to all of the nations of the world. There will be a time where everyone will praise him. At God's timing, all of his children will be surrounded by righteousness. It is a picture of hope and joy that is a comfort to those enduring suffering. Your suffering is not everlasting but you do have God's salvation and righteousness forever.

Prayer for Jerusalem

Isaiah writes a prayer for Jerusalem and its people in Chapter 62. Isaiah promises not to rest due to his love for Zion and how his heart yearns for Jerusalem. He cannot stop praying for Jerusalem due to his desire to see God's promise of glory. Isaiah bemoans the fact that his beloved Jerusalem is known as "The Forsaken City" and "The Desolate Land." He renames Jerusalem as "The City of God's Delight" and "The Bride of God."

Isaiah wants watchmen to pray continually while they keep their eyes looking out for the Lord to raise Jerusalem to glory. He also wants the road to Jerusalem prepared for the return of its people. He calls for the road to be smoothed and boulders removed. Isaiah did additional naming at the end of the chapter for both God's people and Jerusalem. Isaiah names God's people both "The Holy People" and "The People Redeemed by the Lord." Both names can be applied to Jews and

Christians. He gives two more names for Jerusalem: "The Desirable Place" and "The City No Longer Forsake."

Lord's Enemies

Edom was an enemy of Israel that the Jews would recognize. There are multiple times in Israel's history where Edom either attacked Israel or assisted other nations in attacking Israel. Due to this history, Israel would always have a watchman on the wall to ensure that Edom is not approaching. Isaiah foretells that God will trample Israel's enemy Edom. He will destroy them when it is time for Him to avenge His people. He will crush the nations that are the enemies of his people with his anger. God's enemies will stagger and fall when the time is right. You need to be like the watchman in Isaiah 63 and keep your eyes for God who has the power to save. He will announce our salvation from God's enemies when the time is right.

Deliverance

Isaiah praises God for his promise of deliverance. Even though God had not delivered Israel during Isaiah's lifetime, Isaiah is passionate and zealous in his praise of God for what he will do in the future. You need to be like Isaiah and praise God for what He will provide, even when you are in the middle of trouble.

> I will tell of the Lord's unfailing love.
> I will praise the Lord for all he has done.
> I will rejoice in his great goodness to Israel, which he
> had granted according to his mercy and love.
> Isaiah 63: 7 NLT

You need to tell of God's love and praise God for all that he has done. Remember God's mercy and love in all of your actions and words. God is your savior and hopes that you do not betray him. He is betrayed when His children embrace sin. God suffers when you suffer and wants to rescue you. There are times that your suffering is due to your own actions not God's actions. While God could allow you to continuously suffer, He rescues you from sin and provides your needs even when you do not deserve it.

God redeems us from sin because of his love and mercy. It grieves God when we rebel against him. God does not want to be your enemy but people who rebel against him and refuse to recognize God's authority become God's enemy.

God has a magnificent reputation for leading his people and providing their needs. He led Moses out of Egypt. You decide on what God you allow in her life by your actions. He will provide and lead you when you obey Him but He fights you when you rebel against him.

Prayer for Mercy and Pardon

Isaiah asks God for something that we ourselves often ask of God. Isaiah asks for God to show mercy and compassion. Isaiah asks a lot of the same questions that you often hear discouraged people asking of God and about God. God had shown mercy and compassion on Israel in the past and Isaiah asks why it cannot be given again. In Isaiah 63:16, he asks "Lord, why have you allowed us to turn from your path?" Isaiah puts the blame on God for giving us stubborn hearts that caused us not to fear God. He continues to plead for God to return to help His people due to Israel being God's servant and special possession. We have the tendency to think the same questions while continuing to plead for his help while also rationalizing why he should help us. We too often sympathize with Isaiah's wording in Isaiah 63:19,: Sometimes it seems as though we never belonged to you, as though we had never been known as your people.

Society encourages pride in yourself which quickly grows to narcissism. In our current society, it is easy to forget how great and all-consuming God is. Isaiah paints a picture of God in Isaiah 64 that we need to remember more often. If God came down and blessed us with his presence, it would be more than we could handle. When God comes to earth; the mountains would quake, fire would burn the trees and boil the water, and nations would tremble. God is able to do actions that are so much more than our highest expectations.

We are like the tribes of Israel and anger God with our constant sinning. He welcomes those who follow his ways and do good but we are more likely to sin and do evil with our human nature. Then we do as Israel did and refuse to call on God's name nor plead for mercy. God turns away and allows you to turn to sin if you choose just like he did to Israel. God is our father. Isaiah describes God as the potter and we are his clay. He formed us and can mold you when you are open to his instruction. It is important that you remember his role and his power instead of embracing your sinful nature.

Isaiah lived before Jesus and his sacrifice that allows us to get our sins forgiven. Yet he is asking God for exactly what we are able to get due to Jesus's sacrifice: forgiveness of our sins. Isaiah lived at a time when Israel was in a bad state. Cities were destroyed and the temple was burned down. Isaiah could only see destruction and punishment. You can get to a similar state when you embrace sin and are living with the consequences. The question that ends chapter 64 is a question that so many people continue to ask when all they see is destruction "Will you continue to be silent and punish us?" We are luckier than Isaiah in that we have the hope that comes with salvation that Isaiah did not have but did foresee.

Judgment and Final Salvation

The last two chapters of the book are about God's judgment and final salvation for us. We are very much like the people of Judah during Isaiah time. God is ready to respond, be found, and help his people but they were not asking for help, looking for him, nor calling on his name. We are repeating their mistakes. We are being just as rebellious by following our own paths and schemes instead of living God's will. God was patient then and continues to be patient with us.

God's people were worshiping idols and participating in pagan ceremonies. Yet they continued to hold themselves as holier than others and did not consider themself as sinful. They were being hypocrites. We have the tendency to do the same things. God did not let their sins and cannot let our sins go unpunished but he does have a way to pay the cost of sin.

God promises not to stand silent. He had a plan to repay the sins of all people. God's plan does not include destroying all people because God recognizes that there is always a faithful remnant of His people amidst the sinners. He will not destroy everyone because of the few that remain faithful to Him. When He punished Israel with exile, a faithful remnant did exist. God had the plan to keep a few of His people in Israel even during the time of punishment for the tribes.

God planned to bring peace to all places by his promise to restore the Valley of Achor from a Valley of Trouble to its proper use for herds. You need to search for God and He will restore and lead you to peace. God will not save those who do not seek him. People who forsake and forgot Him will be destined for the sword. God clearly compares what He will give to His servant versus what awaits those who do not want to follow Him. God's servant will be fed, rejoice, sing for joy, and be forgiven for earlier evil. In contrast, unbelievers will be thirsty, sad, ashamed, cry in sorrow and despair, and be a curse. While God does not promise an easy life, He does promise to provide your needs and give you what you need for peace. Life will not be easy living in sin, but it will lack the peace that God provides those who seek him.

God told Isaiah His plan to create a new heaven and a new earth. Jerusalem will be a place of happiness and His people will be a source of joy. God will rejoice over Jerusalem and delight in His people in the new heaven and earth. There will be no more weeping and crying there. A beautiful picture is created for this new home. Babies will not die and life will be long. We will build our homes and eat from our own vineyards. We will be able to enjoy our gains and not work in vain. No one will be hurt or destroyed in this new home.

Heaven is God's throne and earth is His footstool. Our human temples and churches are inadequate to hold the power that created both heaven and earth. Everything in heaven and earth belong to God. He created us and we belong to Him. Live with a humble and contrite heart. When you choose your ways instead of God's, you are being prideful and considering yourself above God. God only recognized the sacrifices that were made with proper intention. Now God looks at our intentions when we pray and act. Those whose intent is for praise from the world is not serving God with the proper intention. God will send trouble to those who ignore Him when He speaks and those who deliberately sin.

Isaiah then goes to a message from God concerning how people will treat his servants. He warns those who seek Him will be hated by their own people. People will scoff at you and throw you out due to your loyalty to God. But remember that God is the creator and is creating your new home.

God foretells that Jerusalem will give birth to a son. God promises to restore His nation as he has promised His people. The birthing pain has started but joy will begin when the birth is finished. God tells us to rejoice with Jerusalem and be glad with her. God promises to give Jerusalem a river of peace and prosperity. The wealth of the nations will flow to her.

God promises us that there will be a time when everyone will see His hand of blessing on His servants and anger against His enemies. God will come swiftly and powerfully. He will punish those who sin against Him with the fury of His anger. God's punishment will be done with fire and His sword.

God knows what everyone is doing and thinking. He will gather all nations and people together to have them see His glory. God sends missionaries to all lands to declare His glory to the nations. The missionaries will bring the remnant of people that are faithful to him from every nation. The remnant will be brought to God's holy mountain in Jerusalem as an offering to God. God will appoint some of them to be his priests and Levites.

God assures us that those who serve him with their hearts are always his people and will never disappear. He promises that all humanity will worship Him in the future. Everyone who rebels against him will die and not reach our new home in the new heaven and earth. We are instructed to serve God with our mind, heart and soul. It is easy to rebel in our world and go to the idols of our world due to our own prideful nature. It takes deliberate choice to do God's will in your lives. It is important that you focus on the image of your future with God in the new heaven and earth that he is creating for us while you serve him now.

Chapter 10

THE CROSS REFERENCES
FOR THE BOOK OF ISAIAH
AND CONCLUSION

I saiah has cross references with verses in both the Old Testament and New Testament. Isaiah prophesied during the reigns of king Uzziah, Jotham, Ahaz, and Hezekiah. 2 Chronicles and 2 Kings provides more details about these Kings' reigns. Hosea and Micah were prophets at the same time. This causes some cross references with some of the verses' in their books.If you are reading Isaiah in a Chronological bible, you will find it mixed with parts of 2 Kings, 2 Chronicles, Proverbs, Psalms, and Micah. When you look at the connections in Isaiah, 2 Chronicles, and 2 Kings, it gives a detailed picture of the events on which Isaiah prophesied for the kings that lived during his lifetime.

Isaiah is widely referenced or alluded to in the New Testament which is not a surprise when you consider that Isaiah is an in-depth detailed prediction of Jesus and his ministry. Some of the specific details that are fulfilled or mentioned in the New Testament are:

- Therefore, the Lord himself will give you a sign: See, the virgin will conceive, have a son, and name him Immanuel. Isaiah 7:14

- A voice of one crying out: Prepare the way of the Lord in the wilderness, make a straight highway for our God in the desert. Isaiah 40:3
- But in the future he will bring honor to the way of the sea, to the land east of the Jordan, and to Galilee of the nations. Isaiah 9:1
- Yet he himself bore our sicknesses, and he carried our pains, but we in turn regarded him stricken, struck down by God, and afflicted. But he was pierced because of our rebellion, crushed because of our iniquities, punishment for our peace was on him, and we are healed by his wounds. We are went astray like sheep, we have turned to our way; and the Lord has punished him for the iniquity of us all. Isaiah 53:4-6
- This is my servant; I strengthen him, this is my chosen one; I delight in him. I have put my Spirit on him; he will bring justice to the nations. He will not cry out or shout or make his voice heard in the streets. Isaiah 42:1-2
- And he replied: Go! Say to these people: Keep listening, but do not understand; keep looking, but do not perceive. Isaiah 6:9
- The Lord said: These people approach me with their speeches to honor me with lip-service—yet their hearts are far from me, and human rules direct their worship of me. Isaiah 29:13
- I will bring them to my holy mountain and let them rejoice in my house of prayer. Their burnt offerings and sacrifices will be acceptable on my altar for my house will be called a house of prayer for all nations. Isaiah 56:7
- Therefore I will give him the many as a portion, and he will receive the mighty as spoil, because he willingly submitted to death and was counted among the rebels, yet he bore the sin of many and interceded for the rebels. Isaiah 53:12
- He says, "It is not enough for you to be my servant raising the tribes of Jacob and restoring the protected ones of Israel. I will

also make you a light for the nations, to be my salvation to the ends of the earth. Isaiah 49:6

- The Spirit of the Lord God is on me, because the Lord has anointed me to bring good news to the poor. He has sent me to heal the brokenhearted, to proclaim liberty to the captives and freedom to the the prisoners, to proclaim the year of the Lord's favor, and the day of our God's vengeance; to comfort all who mourn, to provide for those who mourn in Zion; to give them a crown of beauty instead of ashes, festive oil instead of mourning, and splendid clothes instead of despair. And they will be called righteous trees, planted by the Lord to glorify him. Isaiah 61:1-3

- He was oppressed and afflicted, yet he did not open his mouth. Like a lamb led to the slaughter and like a sheep silent before her shearers, he did not open his mouth. Isaiah 53:7

- Paul uses Isaiah's word multiple times in his letter to Rome.

- On that day the root of Jesse will stand as a banner for the peoples. The nations will look to him for guidance, and his resting place will be glorious. Isaiah 11:10

- he will destroy death forever. The Lord God will wipe away the tears from every face and remove his people's disgrace from the whole earth, for the Lord has spoken. Isaiah 25:8

- He was assigned a grave with the wicked, but he was with a rich man at his death, because he had done no violence and had not spoken deceitfully. Isaiah 53:9

- For a child will be born for us, a son will be given to us, and the government will be on his shoulders. He will be named Wonderful Counselor, Mighty God, Eternal Father, Prince of Peace. Isaiah 9:6

These are only a few of the verses in Isaiah that are referenced in the New Testament and some of them are referenced several times.

Both Peter and Paul show that the book of Isaiah was well known by the Israelites before Jesus's birth.

God set up a plan for our salvation and gave it to Isaiah hundred of years before he was going to put his plan into action. The Israelites had Isaiah's prophecy and were waiting and watching for the fulfillment of the promise. At the same time, they forgot to follow God and serve Him. God gave John a prophecy of Jesus's second coming. John wrote that prophecy in Revelation in the early 90 B.C. Let's not repeat the same mistake. Focus on your relationship with God and trust Him with everything while you serve Him. The book of Isaiah shows that God has the plan for our salvation and new home. He knows the timing even though we do not.

Printed in the United States
by Baker & Taylor Publisher Services